Dedicated
to those
who produce food

CONTENTS

ACKNOWLEDGEMENTS

The major portion of the present work, which I wish to present to the esteemed readers, is an outcome carried out during my PhD programme in G.B. Pant University of Agriculture and Technology, Pantnagar under the guidance and supervision of Dr. T.S. Bhogal, Chairman of my Advisory Committee. Without his persistent encouragement, it would have been very hard for me to complete the task.

It is my extreme pleasure to express my heartfelt gratitude to Dr. S.K. Tewari, Professor, Department of Agricultural Economics for developing my concepts and support related to study.

No less is my gratitude to Dr.V.P.S. Arora, Professor, Department of Agricultural Economics and Dean College of Agri-Business Management, Pantnagar to provide the valuable suggestions whenever I needed. I am also thankful to Dr. S.J. Amdekar, Department of Statistics, Mathematics and Computer Science to solve the problems related to statistical methodology.

I wish to express my deep sense of gratitude to Dr. Leena Bhattacharya, Department of Food and Nutrition, College of Home Science and Dr. Gurumukh Singh, Professor, Department of Food Science and Technology, College of Agriculture to provide me the data and basic informations related to food and nutrition aspects.

I am highly thankful to Dr. Ajay Kumar Gauraha, Associate Professor, Indira Gandhi Agricultural University, Raipur, Dr. Prasoon Mathur, Research Fellow, NCAP, ICAR, Pusa and Dr. Shekhar Varshney, Research Fellow, Department of Plant Pathology, G.B. Pant University of Agriculture and Technology, Pantnagar and my colleague Dr. Shalendra for their valuable suggestions.

I pay regards to my supporting senior, juniors and batchmates in department for their help and encouragement during my stay at Pantnagar. I cannot forget their moral support to prepare the model on "food security" which bagged the first prize in *kisan mela* during my chairmanship of the Agricultural Economics Association and Planning Forum, Pantnagar.

The man, who developed the interest in economics and taught me this subject since I was in 6th class, is my father Dr. R.P.S. Rana, who has also contributed to a wide range of publications in different area of economics. I am highly indebted to my father as he not only gave me the idea to do the work on food security while selecting the area for PhD research but also provided me very useful literature to formulate the problem. Space is very small to my desired extent which I owe to my loving mother to provide me the continuous encouragement throughout my life. I am in immense pleasure and feel lucky to get the supporting in-laws, my wife Ms. Jyoti Singh and two-year old son who shared my pains during the writing of this book. I am also thankful to Shri Vijay Kumar Gupta, Publisher, M.D. Publications Pvt. Ltd., New Delhi for excellent production of the book.

Above all, I bow my head to Almighty God who always have been provided me enough patience and energy to face any difficult situation during the study.

PREFACE

The right to food is as good as right to life. Hence, right to food qualifies to become a fundamental right across the nations. Given the importance of food for human life and the complexities of the issues related to it, food security has been a much discussed subject in different National and International forums.Way back in the year 1975, an important early step by FAO was the establishment of the Global Information and Warning System on Food and Agriculture for generating advance information about the possible food emergencies in different parts of the world, so that preventive measures could be taken for the vulnerable communities and areas.

The World Food Summit, held in November 1996, was the first global gathering at the highest political level to focus on food security. The Rome declaration pledged to achieve the food security for all and to eradicate hunger in all countries with a view to reduce the number of undernourished people half to their present level by 2015. The nations has committed itself to eradicate hunger during the world food summit and accordingly taken steps to reduce hunger through various programmes and schemes. However, it is a right of the citizens to ensure that efforts to reach these goals are being made.

The Government provides the access to food to the vulnerable section of the society by Public Distribution System, nutrition and employment programmes. The market mechanism to the large extent also ensures access to food to the people. However, food insecurity still persists in the segment of society falling below the poverty line. This section of the society is under-privileged, less voiced and deprived from the access to food mainly due to the lack of purchasing power. The question now arises how to ensure food security. The answer is that it is the employment to every citizen which may gurantee the food security, for which there should be the provision of "Right to Work" and efforts should be to rely on providing the means to **"hunt the fish rather than to give the fish"** to the vulnerable section of the society. The schemes by Government to provide 100 days of employment guarantee at minimum wages in a year is a good step in ensuring the "Right to Work" interlinking to the "Right to Food" provided it is implemented efficiently. These schemes need to be backed by legal status to prevent the starvation deaths in the country. Besides, our business community should also come forward with maximum employment creation to other sections of society giving due weightage to the poor segment of population.

After India's Independence in 1947, the country faced two major economic challenges: achieving food security and allev*ia*ting poverty. In a country which relies predominantly on agriculture, the logical choice was to promote growth in agriculture to meet both of these challenges. At the macro level, food supply in the country should have satisfactory growth rate commensurate with the population growth. The level of food supply should be matched with food requirement of country rather than the food demand which is necessary to provide the food to all people as per balanced diet norms. The demand is determined mainly by the market system and subject to interchange while the food requirement is valued on the basis of energy (calorie) need of the individuals and is constant for a particular age group. The present work is based on the premises that the gap between food supply and food requirement is a better indicator of the food security level than the usually adopted supply demand gap. The consideration of requirement rather than the demand motivated me to name this book "**Food for All**".

The dynamics of food security can be best perceived, when it is analyzed in different dimensions and perspectives. The concept of food security undergoes a change with the stage of development reached by the society and in developing country like India, the food security is seen as making available minimum quantity of food grains to the entire population. Need less to say that the Indian population is predominantly vegetarian and in their diets, cereals dominate in food expenditure and considered as major source of calories. Also, a recognized role of pulses to supplement the quality proteins in vegetarian diet cannot be neglected. This is the reason that guided me to estimate the requirement of cereals and pulses separately.

As calorie requirements vary across the age groups of population, the traditional method of calculating food requirement based on per capita norm suffers from the problem of averaging and thus may give a value wide of the true food requirement. Hence, as a first step, the present study attempts to estimate the population by different age groups with the help of the population projections at state level. Thereafter, the separate food grains requirement on the basis of age groups has been estimated and summed up to project the total food grains requirement for the year 2005-06 and 2010-11. So far as I am aware, there is no other book is available which deals the estimation of food requirement by the age groups. The second important aspect of this book is the estimation of the projections of production and per capita per day availability of food grains at three levels *viz.* pessimistic, expected and optimistic levels for the same years. Attempts has also been made to project the estimates of food grains storage requirement separately for cereals and pulses for the forcasted production at expected range level.

In most of the books, the chapter on methodology is always avoided or given briefly. My wish to include this chapter is to make all the adopted procedures, including self developed concepts, transparent which may be helpful to correct the errors, if any. Secondly, it would be helpful for the institutions and people dealing with the studies of food security recommending and adopting the same forecasting procedures.

The present work attempts to throw insights into the different aspects of the future food security situation of all major states *via* carrying out the projections of the supply and requirement of food grains separately for cereals and pulses. The estimated projections will also have an important role on policy decisions for food grains covering different aspects like infrastructure, storage, marketing etc. I hope this book would be helpful to evolve a national policy to make a balanced approach between food security and agricultural planning linking food grains production and requirement of our population.

Constructive suggestions for improvement and corrections of errors, if any, will be gladly and gratefully received, highly appreciated and carefully considered.

Gajendra Singh

(GAJENDRA SINGH)

CHAPTER 1

INTRODUCTION

1.1 CONCEPT OF FOOD SECURITY

The concept of food security has been evolved in last quarter of 20th century, and has been an important issue of discussion in number of world conferences convened by the UNO in the decade of 1990's. An important early step in improving world security was the establishment of the global information and early warning system on food and agriculture in FAO* in 1975 which helps the community to prepare in advance to meet the food emergencies. The basic idea behind the food security is to ensure adequate supplies of food to the world people at all times, irrespective of climate or harvests, social status or income.

---

*Food and Agriculture Organization (FAO) is one of the largest specialized agency in the UN System founded in 1945 with a mandate to raise levels of nutrition, improving agricultural productivity, to make better the conditions of rural population and contribute to the growth of the world economy. To serve the mandate, the FAO activities mainly comprise to put information within reach i.e. to serve as a knowledge network, sharing policy expertise to achieve rural development and hunger alleviation goals, providing a meeting place for nations to come together to build common understanding and bringing knowledge to the field projects to make sure to achieve the goals. The objective of FAO is to work and make efforts to achieve the food security for all. India is a member of FAO.

The food security is considered at global, national, regional, state, household and individual level and there are many agencies and institutions which have defined the concept and definitions of food security. The concept of food security has been undergoing refinement during the past many years. The food security defined in the World Food Summit, 1974, means that "availability at all times of adequate world food supplies of basic foodstuffs to sustain a steady expansion of food consumption and to offset fluctuations in production and prices". In 1983, FAO expanded its concept of food security to include securing access by vulnerable people to available supplies. The definition implies that the "all people at all times have both physical and economic access to the basic food they need".

In 1986, the World Bank in its report "Poverty and Hunger" focused on the temporal dynamics of food insecurity and slightly modified this concept which indicated that the food security is "access by all people at all times to enough food for an active and healthy life. Its essential elements are the availability of food and the ability to acquire it". It means that in order to enjoy food security, there must be a provision of adequate food at all the times which also to be accessed physically and economically by all people irrespective of fact that whether they are rich or poor, male or female and old or young.

In 1996, World Food Summit adopted also one more complex definition which implies that "Food security, at the individual, household, national, regional and global levels, when all people, at all times, have physical and economic access to sufficient, safe and nutritious food to meet their dietary needs and food preferences for an active and healthy life". There has been refinement in this food security definition in the report of

"The State of Food Insecurity 2001" which means that "a situation that exists when all people, at all times, have physical, social and economic access to sufficient, safe and nutritious food that meets their dietary needs and food preferences for an active and healthy life".

United States Agency for International Development (USAID) incorporated fundamental concepts of four global governance organizations to comprise the definition as "When all people at all time have both physical and economic access to sufficient food to meet their dietary needs for a productive and healthy life."

A more elaborative definition of food security provided by Dr. M.S. Swaminathan, a renowned Indian Agricultural Scientist closely associated with Green Revolution, which included food and water both, is given as "providing physical and economic access to balanced diets and safe drinking water to all people at all times".

The concept given by the Centre for Studies in Food Security Ryerson University in Canada, states that food security is a condition in which all people at all times can acquire safe, nutritionally adequate and personally acceptable foods that are accessible in a manner that maintains human dignity. It requires attention to the production and supply of adequate quality and quantity of food, and people's ability to acquire those foods. Briefly, the concept included the five principles, namely the availability, accessibility, acceptability, adequacy and agency in which the fifth one, "agency", reflects focus on governance and systems for enabling citizen participation.

The concept of food security under goes to change with the stage of development reached by the society, and at present stage the food security in India may be visualized to make available minimum quantity of food grains to the entire population. Food grains are important in Indian context as our first problem is to reduce hunger, therefore trend in per capita supply of food grains is always considered as an indicator of improvements in the food security. Food security and hunger are different and opposite concepts as, food security indicates the availability of food, while hunger is a state of food insecurity situation which results due to the non-availability of food. The famines out come in particular area due to natural disasters also leads to hunger and state of food insecurity situation.

The increased availability of food is a necessary condition in food deficit countries to achieve the food security which should be matched by reduction in poverty to ensure economic access for the poor, as well as the physical access to food by all people at all times both in quantity and quality to meet their nutritional requirement enough for an active and healthy life. In the early 1980s, there was a shift in thinking about food security influenced by the concept of food entitlement or the view of food as a basic right. The household and individual food security is different and a household is food secure only when it has access to food for all its members. An active and healthy life for a particular household or an individual is only possible when there is also access to the other basic services like water supply and a hygienic environment and knowledge of personal hygiene so that the food can be efficiently consumed. Further, within household a individual member even may not be the food secure, for example, in many societies particularly in rural areas the women even do not take food with the men and takes the food only after the male members have consumed the food, irrespective of the fact that this remaining food is sufficient or insufficient for her. Thus, wife of a poor man particularly in developing countries is most undernourished human being in the present world.

The physical and economic access is always analyzed in respect of Public Distribution System and poverty levels of the household respectively, therefore the establishment of an efficient Public Distribution System and eradication of household poverty are the important considerations to achieve the food security.

1.2 MEANING OF FOOD INSECURITY, UNDER-NOURISHMENT, VULNERABILITY AND NUTRITIONAL STATUS

It is always considered that the poverty is the major determinant of food insecurity. The meaning of food insecurity, undernourishment, vulnerability and nutritional status is also given by the Committee on World Food Security* in Twenty Fifth Session. The term undernourishment in the Summit implied for those persons whose food consumption level is inadequate in terms of calories consumed relative to requirements on a continuing basis. The food insecurity implied to exist when people lack access to sufficient amounts of safe and nutritious food and not consuming the food required for normal growth and development, for an active and healthy life. Food insecurity may be either chronic or transitory. When food insecurity is chronic, there is under-nourishment. The vulnerability refers to full range of factors that place people at risk of becoming food insecure, including those factors that affect their ability to cope while the nutritional status refers that physiological state of people that results from a combination of food intake, care practices and health and sanitation conditions. Further in the summit, it was extended

*The Committee on World Food Security (CFS) serves as a forum in the United Nations System for review and follow-up of policies concerning world food security. India is a member of CFS.

that for the specific groups of people, the nature of vulnerability differs according to the kinds of food insecurity involved which are of three kinds, namely, chronic food insecurity, lean season or cyclical food insecurity and transitory food insecurity. The chronic food insecurity implies the situation in which the food insecure individual or group is or has been regularly consuming somewhat less than the minimum needed over a considerable period of time. The lean season or cyclical food insecurity implies the situation in which the food insecure have enough to eat in the immediate post-harvest period, but do not have enough to eat for a certain period before the next harvest while transitory food insecurity implies the situation in which food insecure people experience variations in access to food that provoke deterioration in their food intake at certain times to the point that their health and well-being is endangered.

In India, all the three types of food insecurity exist. The first type of food insecurity i.e., the chronic food insecurity is primarily associated with continuously inadequate diet due to poverty levels. The occurrence of starvation deaths due to chronic hunger among the vulnerable section of the society has been a common feature in India.

The Planning Commission reports indicate that in 1999-2000 there is about 26.10% of population below the poverty line. The lean season or cyclical food insecurity may exists among those farm households which have inadequate cultivable land to fulfill there food needs. The situation becomes worse when these farmers household goes for the distress sale for the produce. In many poor countries there is seasonal hunger, usually in the months just before the coming harvest. The third type of food insecurity exists mostly in states which face the floods, droughts and other natural disasters. Examples of these states are Orissa, Assam, Rajasthan etc.

The identification of the underfed and undernourished is necessary to provide the adequate food. For this purpose, governments at the 1996 World Food Summit committed themselves to the development of Food Insecurity and Vulnerability Information and Mapping Systems (FIVIMS). FIVIMS is essentially a database involving network of information and mapping system, which assembles detailed information about the people who are food insecure and their location on the basis of factors such as agriculture, nutrition, health, education, social welfare, economic well-being, employment opportunities and social environment to develop a data base, to identify pockets of food insecurity.

1.3 FOOD POPULATION RELATION SHIP AND GENDER ISSUES IN FOOD SECURITY

In 1994, the International Conference on Population and Development in Cairo highlighted the linkage between the population growth and food production, and the need to evolve global measures to satisfy the ever growing food needs. In 1996, the World Food Summit at Rome which took place at a time of growing international concern over slow growth in food production and expanding population, concentrated to the fight for food security. The India is the first country to adopt a national population control programme in 1952, with an objective to stabilize population at a level the national economy could absorb. After 1952, sharp declines in death rates were, however, not accompanied by a similar drop in birth rates. The India 's current annual increase in population of 15.5 million is large enough to neutralize any efforts to conserve the resource endowment and may soon make it the most populous country of the world; over taking China by 2045 AD. (National Population Policy Report, 2000). A primary condition for food security is the stabilization of population and in India, food security in the long term will depend partly on slowing population growth in the coming decades. In eighties, the annual growth rate of food grains was about 3.5% which fallen to 1.7% which is just about equal to population growth rate and implying a stagnant per capita production level. The growth rate in agricultural output is composed of growth rate in area and growth rate in yield. There are limits to increase the agricultural production through increase in area as land is a fixed factor of production. Naturally, increase in agricultural output will have to come almost wholly from growth in yield.

It is widely evident that there is unequal access to food in the country across regions, social and economic classes, gender and age groups of people. The gender dimension of food security received attention at the World Conference on Women held at Beijing in 1995. The principle of social access, with reference to women and marginalized communities was added to the concept of food security. The unequal access across gender and age groups is a social problem. Women play a pivotal role in securing and preparing food for the family and in spite of this fact when the food is inadequate for the family consumption, men get preference over women and boys get preference over girls. Women during pregnancy and lactation period have specific nutrient requirements which determine their nutritional status. The women in developing countries perform double duty i.e. at home preparing meals, and at work place act as labour. In many societies particularly in rural India specific needs of women are not recognized and priority is given to feeding other members of the family. It has been seen that preference for son is more in Indian culture and daughters are always regarded as burden and a responsibility to the parents. The female babies also receive less medical care than their brothers. Rural women are producers of food, traders, and family caretakers and plays important roles in their communities as well as in national economies. A household can be comparatively be more food secure in case if the women is able to exercise greater control over the decisions involving the disposal of household income as she will spend a greater proportion of household income on food compared with men. Especially in rural areas, it has been seen that as women engage more in income-earning activities or participate in husbands work then husbands partially withdraw from work and enjoys more leisure at the expense of their hard-working wives. In these conditions besides increasing the food production, the social environment also needs to be changed along with the more opportunities to increase the family income.

1.4 NATURAL DISASTERS AND FOOD SECURITY

It has been observed that nearly all kinds of natural disasters like floods, cyclones, droughts or famines, earthquakes, landslides, avalanches etc occur in our country. People lose access to food in times of natural calamities. Natural disasters like cyclones and flood can be predicted to some extent on the basis of past records but the disaster like earth quake cannot be predicted as it is an uncertainty.

In the history of famines, there are numerous instances when one famine year was followed by another lean year. Sometime a lean year (as happened in 1941) preceded a full blooded famine. In these situations, the economy of farmers is ruined and the small and marginal farmers are the worst victims. The sustaining power as well as the working capital of farmers is completely lost due to the loss of crops which aggravate the food security problem. The dreadful Bengal famine of 1942-43, accompanied by World War II, led to creation of food department (December,1942). In July 1943, the Central Government appointed the food grain policy committee presided by Mr. Vigour, which for the first time in the history of Indian administration prepared scientific and logically reasoned charter for food administration. Looking at the recurring arrival of drought in the last century, it can be observed that there were seven drought years between 1901 and 1925; two drought years between 1926 and 1950; six drought years between 1951 and 1975 and nine drought years between 1976 and 2000. The year of 2002 is the first drought year of the 21st century and it is said that this year has face the worst drought since 1987. If the trend of the last century is any indication, we may have to face many more drought years in coming decades. Due to deficient rainfall in dought periods and increasing use of ground water, the water level is falling every year.

The experiences of famines results the Government of India to formulate the famine relief policy in 1878 for the first time. On the basis of lessons learnt from 1987 and other droughts in the country, the Government revised its guidelines in 1989 on drought management. The current policy emphasizes more on mitigation and preventive measures. The Government has also identified areas prone to droughts, which are being continually treated under various programmes.

The United Nations declared the decade of 1990-1999 as the International Decade for the Natural Disasters Reduction (IDNDR). The Government of India is observing the current decade as the National Decade for Disaster Reduction. The Government also observes 29th October, the day on which a super cyclone had hit Orissa in 1999, as the National Day for Disaster Reduction. There are many initiatives has been taken at national and state level with an objective to mitigate disasters.

One of the initiative in the last decade is the setting up of a High Powered Committee (HPC) on Disaster Management Plans. There are five sub-groups to look into the various aspects of disaster management constituted under the HPC like water and climate related hazards, geological hazards, chemical/ industrial /nuclear/disasters, accident related disasters and biological disasters. The Government established a National Committee for Disaster Management with the objective to suggest the institutional and legislative measures for strengthening the disaster management structure of the country. Under the joint efforts of UNDP and Government of India, a programme on Disaster Risk Management (DRM) was designed with the objective to assist the states and regions which are prone to natural disasters. The other initiatives are the preparation of Hazard Mapping and Vulnerability Assessment of Buildings, National Programme on Monitoring and Impact Assessment of Natural Hazards, Programme on Enhancing Emergency Response (PEER), Strengthening of Information Technologies and Disaster Warning System (DWS).

The availability of food at national or regional level does not ensure food security to any particular disaster affected area as what surplus is available at national or regional level may not be accessed by natural disaster affected people of that region i.e., godowns may be full with food grains in one region but in spite of this people may be starving because of lack of access of food in another disaster affected area. To face the situations like drought, there is a need to come forward with urgent schemes for relief and rehabilitation. Immediate release of food grains from godowns of agencies dealing with food security should be ordered and sent to all the affected regions along with cash funds and "food for work" must be started for agricultural workers and poor peasants with the help of local *panchayats*. In order to avoid acute food shortages due to wide spread crop failures or natural disasters, appropriate national stock policies maintaining minimum safe level of food at proper locations with proper public distribution network needs to be designed.

1.5 PUBLIC DISTRIBUTION SYSTEM AND FOOD SECURITY FOR THE POOR

During the last two decades, Indian studies have shifted their focus to food security concern also at the household and individual level. The efficacy of any food security at household level and individual level can be judged only with reference to the Public Distribution System(PDS) through which it is translated into action. The PDS has its origin during the second World War period and it has emerged as an effective instrument to support the food security of poor households *via* supplying the essential commodities like food grains mainly rice and wheat, kerosene, edible oil, sugar etc which are distributed through a network of retail outlets known as Fair Price Shops (FPS). PDS is operated with a net work of about 4.83 lakhs Fair Price Shops, under the joint responsibility of the Central and the State Government. The distribution and operational responsibilities like distribution of food grains through FPS, allocation with in states, identification of families below poverty line, issue of ration cards, supervision and monitoring etc are shared by the State Government while the Central Government under takes the responsibility for procurement, storage, transportation and bulk allocation of food grains. The Central Government *via* Food Corporation of India (FCI) procures and stocks food grains which are released every month to states for distribution through the Fair Price Shops at uniform Central Issue Price (CIP) which is much below than the economic cost. The economic cost is incurred due to procurement, storage, transport and distribution and the difference between the CIP and economic cost is called consumer subsidy which is borne by the Central Government.

In 1992, the Government introduced a new system named Revamped Public Distribution system for the lower strata of society in a few selected areas. A revised scheme for distribution known as Targeted Public Distribution System (TPDS), with a view to focus on the poor, has also been introduced from June 1997 which envisages a two tier system of delivery to households Below Poverty Line (BPL) and Above Poverty Line (APL) with BPL families receiving food grains at heavily subsidized price.

Although, a very high subsidy is allocated through the targeted PDS, but in spite of this it is always argued at state level that the allocation of ration of 10 kg per month per BPL family is inadequate for the one month consumption and the scale of this ration should be increased. Keeping in view, the allocation of food grains to BPL families increased from 10 kg to 20 kg per family per month at 50% of economic cost w.e.f. 1st April 2000 which further increased to 25 kgs w.e.f. July, 2001 and 35 kg per family per month w.e.f. April, 2002. The allocation to APL is at the economic cost and has also been increased to 35 kg per family per month w.e.f. 1st April 2002.

At the policy level, the agencies dealing with food distribution has always intention to provide the better services of delivery of food to the poor, but inspite of this often there is criticism due to inadequate coverage and implementation of these services at grass root level.

A number of studies have been conducted on PDS which focuses the inadequate coverage of PDS, leakages and inefficiencies of the respective agencies. The basic question, which needs to be probed, is whether PDS purchases are able to help the poor. Due to lack of purchasing power among the lower income groups a section of the population cannot even consume the standard amount of cereals. Besides, the protein gap in lower and middle income groups is more pronounced, due to high prices of pulses. The public distribution system has been established with the aim making accessible to the middle and lower groups, certain essential commodities at a price lower the market price. But in reality, the actual needy sections of the population could not be benefited appreciably due to various reasons and to deal these issues, there is a need to have a good practical approach especially at grass root level alongwith development of welfare schemes. In fact, increasingly higher production of food combined with a generalized public distribution is no guarantee for ensuring food security to the poor segment of the population unless and until there is an efficient distribution network of food. Therefore, the objective of the PDS is to ensure that the poor actually get the services making physical access of essential commodities.

The Food Corporation of India maintains buffer stock of food grains which built up in the year of good production and helps to maintain food security system of our country in the years of lean production and natural disasters. The other objectives is to ensure the monthly supply of food grains through the PDS / welfare schemes and stabilization of market open prices.The buffer norms are revised and finalized from time to time by the government which is based on the realistic requirement of food grains under the existing and new schemes. A part of the food subsidy also goes toward meeting the carrying cost of buffer stock. The maintaining of buffer stock which involves the carrying cost results the food subsidy when added to the consumers subsidy. The Government reviews the food grains stocks held in the central pool by FCI, state government and their agencies on monthly basis and it is ensured that the stocks of rice and wheat in the Central Pool is sufficient to meet the requirement under targeted Public Distribution system(TPDS) and other welfare schemes. The minimum buffer norms and actual stock of rice and wheat under the Central Pool which also includes the revised buffer norms for the remaining 10th five year (i.e from 01.04.2005 to 01.01.2006) is presented in the Table 1.1.

Table 1.1 Stock position of Wheat & Rice in the Central Pool and minimum buffer norms from 01.04.2005 to 01.01.2006 (in lakh tonnes)

As on	*Wheat*		*Rice*		*Total*	
	Actual Stock	*Minimum Buffer Norms*	*Actual Stock*	*Minimum Buffer Norms*	*Actual Stock*	*Minimum Buffer Norms*
01.04.2002	260.39	40.00	249.12	118.00	509.51	158.00
01.04.2003	156.45	40.00	171.57	118.00	328.02	158.00
01.04.2004	69.31	40.00	130.69	118.00	200.00	158.00
01.04.2005	40.66	40.00	133.41	122.00	174.07	162.00
01.07.2005	144.54	171.00	100.71	98.00	245.25	269.00
01.10.2005	102.90	110.00	48.49	52.00	151.39	162.00
01.01.2006	61.88	82.00	126.41	118.00	188.29	200.00

Under TPDS, the ratio of Rice and Wheat under APL and BPL category was streamlined w.e.f. 1st August, 2005 accordingly with the food habits of different states, however there is no change in the overall allocation to States/UTs.

Source :- (Table 1.1 to 1.4 and 1.6) Annual Report 2005-06, Ministry of Consumer Affairs, Food and Public Distribution, Department of Food and Public Distribution and Website : fcamin.nic.in/dfpd./(Department of Food and Public Distribution)

Poverty is the major determinant of food insecurity. The chronic food insecurity is primarily associated with continuously inadequate diet due to poverty levels. The occurrence of starvation deaths due to chronic hunger among the vulnerable section of the society has been a common feature in India. The Planning Commission reports indicate that in 1999-2000 there is about 26.10% of population below the poverty line. A National Sample Survey points out that about 5% of the population sleeps in a country without two square meals a day. In these conditions, the PDS and other government welfare schemes may be the lifelines for impoverished families. Keeping in view, the schemes like Antoydaya Anna Yojana (AAY) were introduced with the aim to make the TPDS more effective in reducing the hunger among the poorest segment of population. Under the AAY (launched on 25th Dec., 2000) the identified families are being provided food grains at rates below the rate charged for the BPL families. At present (2005-06) the scheme has coverage of about 2.5 crore households. The details of the other main welfare schemes related to allocation of food grains has also been arranged in the Table 1.2

Table 1.2 Details of main welfare schemes run by the Government in brief

Name of Scheme		*Main features of the Scheme*
Mid Day Meal Scheme	1.	The scheme was launched by the Ministry of HRD (Department of Education) w.e.f 15th August, 1995 in primary schools in Employment Assurance Scheme (EAS)/ earlier Revamped Public Distribution System(RPDS) covering students (Class I-V) in the Government Primary Schools / Primary Schools aided by Govt. and the Primary Schools run by local bodies.

2. The Foodgrains (wheat and rice) are supplied free of cost and in drought affected areas the mid day meal is distributed in summer vacations also. Under the scheme the allocation is decided by Department of Elementary Education and Literacy and accordingly FCI releases food grains to States/UTs at BPL rates.

Wheat Based Nutrition Programme

1. This Scheme is implemented by the Department of Women & Child Development, M/o Human Resource Development.
2. The foodgrains allotted under this Scheme are utilized by the States/UTs under Integrated Child Development Scheme (ICDS) for providing nutritious/ energy food to children below 6 years of age and expectant /lactating women.

Scheme for Supply of food Grains to Hostels /Welfare Institutions (5% of BPL allocation)

1. This scheme was introduced during 2002-03 with a view to meet the requirement of Hostels /Welfare Institutions *viz.* N.G.Os/ Charitable Institutions which help the shelterless/homeless poor and other categories not covered under TPDS or under any other Welfare Schemes.

2. In this scheme, an additional allocation of food grains (rice and wheat) equal to 5% of the BPL allocation of each State/UT is made to States/UTs at BPL rates.

National Food for Work Programme

1. National Food for Work Programme, launched from 13.10.2004, is being implemented in 150 most backward districts of the country to generate the supplementary wage employment and

providing of food security through creation of need based economic, social and community assets.

2. The scheme is to provide 100 days of employment at minimum wages for at least one able-bodied person from each household in the country. Most of the backward district, which would benefit from the scheme are in the tribal belts.

Annapurana

1. This scheme was launched by the Ministry of Rural Development in 2000-2001. Indigent senior citizens or 65 years of age or above who though eligible for old age pension under the National Old Age Pension Scheme (NOAPS) but are not getting the pension are covered under the Scheme.

2. 10 kgs. of foodgrains per person per month are supplied free of cost under the scheme.

Sampoorna Gramin Rojgar Yojana(SGRY)

1. The Prime Minister on 15.8.2001 announcedthe introduction of a Universal Food for Work Programme to be called "Sampoorna Gramin Rozgar Yojana" in all the States/UTs for organizing various employment generation programmes. The Ministry of Rural Development launched the scheme on 25.9.2001.

2. Under the Scheme, 50 lakh tonnes of food grains is to be allotted to the States/UTs free of cost by Ministry of Rural Development. Ministry of Rural Development reimburse the cost of food grains at economic cost prevailing at the time.

Grain Bank Scheme

The scheme has recently been transferred to Ministry of Consumer Affairs, Food & Public Distribution from Ministry of Tribal Affairs. The objective of the scheme is to establish Grain Banks in chronically food scarce areas.

Nutritional Programme for Adolesent Girls

1. Nutritional Programme for Adolescent Girls'(NPAG) was launched by the Planning Commission initially for a period of two years i.e. 2002-03 and 2003-04 in identified districts. The scheme is administered by Department of Women and Child Development, Ministry of Human Resource at the Central level while the State/UT Governments implement the scheme.
2. The adolescent girls of age group 11-19 years as identified by weight less than 35 Kg are given free foodgrains @ 6kg. per beneficiary per month initially for a period of three months.irrespective of financial status of the family to which they belong.

Emergency Feeding Programme

1. The scheme for Emergency Feeding Programme was introduced in May, 2001 and is being implemented by Government of Orissa in eight identified Districts covering 2 lakh beneficiaries.

2. It is a food-based intervention programme targeted for old, infirm and destitute persons belonging to BPL households to provide them food security in their distress conditions under which food grains (rice) at BPL rates is being allocated to State Government by Department of Food & Public Distribution @ 6 kgs/beneficiary/ month on the recommendation of Ministry of Social Justice & Empowerment.

The Procurement of food grains is based on the Minimum Support Price (MSP) which is announced by the Central Government with a view to support the farm income of farmers and to stabilize the production. The scheme of decentralized procurement of food grains has also been announced by the Government in 1997-98 with a view to enhance the efficiency of procurement and PDS as well as to encourage local procurement for the benefits of farmers Under this scheme the State Government directly purchase the paddy, wheat and procure the levy rice on behalf of the Government of India. The Central Government undertakes the entire expenditure incurred by the State Governments on the procurement operations as per the approved costing. Eleven states namely West Bengal, Uttar Pradesh, Madhya Pradesh, Chhatisgarh, Uttarakhand, Andaman & Nicobar Islands, Orissa, TamilNadu, Gujarat, Karnataka and Kerala have now undertaken the responsibility of procuring the food grains with in the states and distributing the same to the targeted population under TPDS and other welfare schemes. The Central Government undertakes the entire expenditure incurred by the State Governments on the procurement operations as per the approved costing. The difference between the state specific economic cost and the Central Issue Price is passed on to the state as food subsidy. The amount of food subsidy depends on the level of procurement of food grains and release of same under the TPDS and welfare schemes.

The year wise break up of subsidy released on food grains since 2002-03 to FCI and the states operating the Decentralized procurement scheme is give under Table 1.3.

Table 1.3 Year wise break up of subsidy released on food grains

(In Crores)

Year		*Subsidy released*	
	FCI	*States*	*Total*
2002-03	22674	1502	24176
2003-04	23874	1286	25160
2004-05	23280	2466	25746
2005-06 (as on 10 Feb /06)	17707	2760	20467

The increment of MSP adversely affects the economic access of the poor for the food grains distributed through the PDS. The food security system *via* PDS for the poor households cannot be neglected and MSP is also necessary to support the farm income of farmers as well as the stabilization of production. As both of these are important issues and the Central Government maintains the balance between these two aspects by raising the food subsidy. In the era of liberalization and process of economic reforms initiated in 1991, one of the pressures is to limit the food subsidy which may affect the food security programmes of our country.

The minimum support prices for major agricultural products are announced each year which are fixed after taking into account the recommendations of the Commission for Agricultural Costs and Prices (CACP). The CACP recommends the MSP after taking consideration of many factors like Cost of Production, changes in Input Prices, Input/Output Price Parity, Trends in Market Prices Inter-crop Price Parity, Demand and Supply Situation, Effect on Industrial Cost Structure, Effect on General Price Level, Effect on Cost of Living, International Market Price Situation, Parity between Prices Paid and Prices

Received by farmers (Terms of Trade). Of all the factors, cost of production is the most tangible and important factor.

The MSP of wheat and paddy from 2002-03 to 2006-07 is given under Table 1.4

Table 1.4 MSP of wheat and paddy from 2002-03 to 2006-07

Year	*Wheat*	*Paddy*	
		Common	*Grade –A*
2002-03	620	530*	560*
2003-04	620**	550	580
2004-05	630	560	590
2005-06	640	570	600
2006-07	650***		

* The government approved the payment of special drought relief price of Rs. 20 per quintal for paddy

** The government approved the payment of special drought relief price of Rs. 10 per quintal for wheat

*** In addition the government approved an incentive bonus of Rs. 50 per quintal on wheat procurement over the MSP of Rs. 650 per quintal for the rabi season 2006-07.

1.6 FOOD NUTRITION AND POVERTY IN INDIA

Food security is a necessary but insufficient condition for ensuring nutritional security. The gap between availability and requirement for all the categories of food has lead to micro-nutrient deficiencies among vulnerable sections. The major nutrition public health problems are chronic energy deficiency and under-nutrition, micro-nutrient deficiencies, Anaemia due to iron and folate, Vitamin A deficiency and Iodine Deficiency Disorders.

At lower incomes, the possibility of substituting cereals by high cost calorie food items such as milk, meat,vegetables fruits is rare. As income rises, consumers will diversify their dietary pattern towards more expensive and high quality items. A balanced diet contains different types of foods in adequate quantities and proportions needed for calories, minerals, vitamins and other nutrients . ICMR recommends energy derived from cereals should not be more than 75% of total requirements and pulses can supplement cereals to restore the quality of vegetarian diet as these are rich in lysine. The most effective combination is 4 parts of cereal protein and 1 part of pulses protein. In terms of grains it will be 8 parts of cereals and 1 part of pulses. The replacement of egg, fish or meat (from 50 to 100%) by suitable quantities of pulses has been suggested by the ICMR. Thus pulses production is equally essential in Indian context to fulfill the nutritional gap, mainly observed in lower and middle income groups.

Extensive diet surveys carried out in different parts of country both in rural and urban areas reveals that diets are predominantly based on cereals. It is seen that while the diet of middle income group's people in urban area is fairly satisfactory, the diets of rural people are inadequate in several respects, which may continue to be unfavorable for the coming time unless there is phenomenal improvement in their economic status to afford an adequate diet. Thus poverty is the major determinant, which influences calorie intake and decides the qualitative aspects of the diet depending on the consumption habits of the people.

The term poverty is defined in different countries in different way, but all of them condition the minimum or good life to be obtained in society. Several economists and organizations have given different estimates of poverty. The expert group of Planning Commission has defined poverty line on the basis of nutritional norm of per capita daily intake of 2400 calories in rural areas and 2100 calories for urban areas. A person who fails to obtain this minimum level of calories is being treated as below the poverty line.

Poverty reduction has been the top priority of development endeavors over many years. The poverty levels have declined since the anti-poverty programmes were implemented on a large scale in the early 1980s.Despite the fact that significant progress has been made in improving living standards in our country, about 26.10% people still fall below the poverty line as per the data given by planning commission for the year 1999-2000.

The poverty ratios at the state and national level is given in Table 1.5. The table shows that the incidence of poverty (expressed as the percentage of people below the poverty line) has declined from 54.88 in 1973-74 to 26.10% in 1999-2000. The poverty declined from 56.44 to 49.01% in rural area and from 49.01 to 23.62% during the same period. The poverty has been declined almost in all the states, but it is relatively high in Orissa, Bihar and in northern/eastern states.

Table 1.5 Poverty Ratio at the State Level (percent)

S.	State	*Rural*			*Urban*			*Combined*		
		1973-74	*1993--94*	*1999-2000*	*1973-74*	*1993-94*	*1999-2000*	*1973-74*	*1993-94*	*1999-2000*
1.	Andhra Pradesh	48.41	15.92	11.05	50.61	38.33	26.33	48.86	22.19	15.77
2.	Arunachal Pradesh	52.67	45.01	40.04	36.92	7.73	7.47	51.93	39.35	33.47
3.	Assam	52.67	45.01	40.04	36.92	7.73	7.47	51.21	40.86	36.09
4.	Bihar	62.99	58.21	44.30	52.96	34.50	32.91	61.91	54.96	42.60
5.	Goa	46.85	5.34	1.35	37.69	27.03	7.52	44.26	14.92	4.40
6.	Gujrat	46.35	22.18	13.17	52.57	27.89	15.59	48.15	24.21	14.07
7.	Haryana	34.23	28.02	8.27	40.18	16.38	9.99	35.36	25.05	8.74
8.	Himachal Pradesh	27.42	30.34	3.97	21.32	9.18	4.63	26.39	28.44	7.63

9. Jammu & Kashmir	45.51	30.34	3.97	21.32	9.18	1.98	40.83	25.17	3.48
10. Karnataka	55.14	29.88	17.38	52.53	40.14	25.25	54.47	33.16	20.04
11. Kerala	59.19	25.76	9.38	62.74	24.55	20.27	59.79	25.43	12.72
12. Madhya Pradesh	62.66	40.64	37.06	57.65	48.38	38.44	61.78	42.52	37.43
13. Maharashtra	57.71	37.93	23.72	43.87	35.15	26.81	53.24	36.86	25.02
14. Manipur	52.67	45.01	40.04	36.92	7.73	7.47	49.96	33.78	28.54
15. Meghalya	52.67	45.01	40.04	36.92	7.73	7.47	50.20	37.92	33.87
16. Mizoram	52.67	45.01	40.04	36.92	7.73	7.47	50.32	25.66	19.47
17. Nagaland	52.67	45.01	40.04	36.92	7.73	7.47	50.81	37.92	32.67
18. Orissa	67.28	49.72	48.01	55.62	41.64	42.83	66.18	48.56	47.15
19. Punjab	28.21	11.95	6.35	27.96	11.35	5.75	28.15	11.77	6.16
20. Rajasthan	44.76	26.46	13.74	52.13	30.49	19.85	46.14	27.14	15.28
21. Sikkim	52.67	45.01	40.04	36.92	7.73	7.47	50.86	41.43	36.55
22. Tamil Nadu	57.43	32.48	20.55	49.40	39.77	22.11	54.94	35.03	21.12
23. Tripura	52.67	45.01	40.04	36.92	7.73	7.47	51.00	39.01	34.44
24. Uttar Pradesh	56.33	42.28	31.22	60.09	35.39	30.89	57.07	40.85	31.15
25. West Bengal	73.16	40.80	31.85	34.67	22.41	14.86	63.43	35.66	27.02
26. A&N Island	57.43	32.48	20.55	49.40	39.77	22.11	55.56	34.47	20.99
27. Chandigarh	27.96	11.35	5.75	27.96	11.35	5.75	27.96	11.35	5.75
28. Dadra & Nagar Hav.	46.85	51.95	17.57	37.69	39.93	13.52	46.55	50.84	17.14
29. Daman & Diu	NA	5.34	1.35	NA	27.03	7.52	NA	15.80	4.44
30. Delhi	24.44	1.90	0.40	52.23	16.03	9.42	49.61	14.69	8.23
31. Lakshadweep	59.19	25.76	9.38	62.74	24.55	20.27	59.68	25.04	15.60
32. Pondicherry	57.43	32.48	20.55	49.40	39.77	22.11	53.82	37.40	21.67
All India	56.44	37.27	27.09	49.09	32.36	23.62	54.88	35.97	26.10

NA : Not Available

1. Poverty Ratio of Assam is used for Sikkim, Arunachal Pradesh, Meghalaya, Mizoram, Manipur, Nagaland and Tripura.
2. Poverty Line of Maharashtra and expenditure distribution of Goa is used to estimate poverty ratio of Goa.
3. Poverty Line of Himachal Pradesh and expenditure distribution of Jammu & Kashmir is used to estimate poverty ratio of Jammu &Kashmir.
4. Poverty Ratio of Tamil Nadu is used for Pondicherry and A & N Island
5. Urban Poverty Ratio of Punjab used for both rural and urban poverty of Chandigarh

6. Poverty Line of Maharashtra and expenditure distribution of Dadra & Nagar Haveli is used to estimate poverty ratio of Dadra & Nagar Haveli.
7. Poverty Ratio of Goa is used for Daman & Diu.
8. Poverty Ratio of Kerala is used for Lakshadweep.
9. Urban Poverty Ratio of Rajasthan may be treated as tentative.
10. Estimates on a 30 day recall basis for 1999-2000.

Source* : Planning Commission.
* adopted from website:-indiabudget.nic.in/es2001-02/chapt2002/chap102

1.7 STORAGE OF FOOD GRAINS

Food is a basic human need and availability and satisfactory quality of food depend on the development and integration of marketing chain. Storage is one of the crucial components of this marketing chain and is necessary to meet out the demand of particular agricultural commodity for the rest of the year. The storages play an important role to reduce the losses in quantity and quality of produce, prevention of distress sale by the farmers and creating employment opportunities in the rural areas. In the era of liberalization, the storage facilities is coming to provide a convenient instrument of the credit in the form of ware house receipt against which they can borrow from banks. Storage is practiced by farmers, traders to facilitate marketing and by Government to ensure food security.

Prevention of distress sale is possible only when farmers have the economic strength to retain produce with themselves till the market prices are favorable. There is a felt need in the country to provide the farming community with facilities for scientific storage so that wastage and produce deterioration are avoided and also to enable them to meet their credit requirement without being compelled to sell the produce at a time when the prices are low.

Grain deterioration in storage can be minimized or prevented by keeping the grain dry, cool and free from insects. The principle factors that lead to the proliferation of insects in stored grain are temperature and humidity. Occurrence of mites in stored grain is related to high grain moisture content. Unfortunately, many resource-poor farmers use grain storage structures that are inadequate to protect grain from rain or dampness and rodent or insect infestation.

There are three main agencies in the public sector which are engaged in building large scale storage/warehousing capacity *viz.*, Food Corporation of India(FCI), Central Warehousing Corporation (CWC) and State Warehousing Corporation (SWCs). The Food Corporation of India is the main agency for creation of storage capacity while Central Warehousing Corporation is the second main agency for creation of storage capacity in the country and distribution of food grains. The capacity available with FCI is used mainly for storage of food grains. It has its own godowns and it also hires storage capacity from other sources like CWC, SWCs and private parties. The main functions of the CWC and SWC are to acquire and build warehouses at suitable places and to operate them for storage of agricultural production, fertilizers, and certain other items including industrial goods.

Over a period of time, sizeable scientific storage/ warehousing capacity has been developed by these public sector agencies and they are implementing plans to increase it further through the schemes for godown construction. The state wise storage capacity available with different storage agencies in the country is given in Table 1.6.

Table 1.6 State wise storage capacity available with different storage agencies in the the country

(Figures in Lakh Tonnes)

State	*FCI**	*CWC***	*SWC***	*Others****	*Grand Total*
ANDHRA PRADESH	34.30	14.60	22.58	12.85	84.33
BIHAR	5.22	1.10	2.51	5.49	14.32
GUJRAT	5.66	6.27	2.70	2.25	16.88
HARYANA	21.87	5.20	14.09	15.90	57.06
KARNATAKA	6.06	4.50	9.45	4.31	24.32
KERALA	5.33	1.23	1.93	0.79	9.28
MADHYA PRADESH	5.34	6.02	11.88	5.25	28.49
MAHARASHTRA	15.55	15.49	12.16	13.69	56.89
ORISSA	6.47	1.90	4.07	4.52	16.96
PUNJAB	69.83	7.09	57.31	60.67	194.90
RAJASTHAN	9.05	7.47	13.94	0.03	30.49
TAMILNADU	8.54	6.70	6.27	24.33	45.84
UTTAR PRADESH	25.26	11.17	29.13	14.95	80.51
WEST BENGAL	10.08	7.64	2.17	1.31	21.20
JAMMU & KASHMIR	1.12	0.00	0.00	1.49	2.61
HIMACHAL PRADESH	0.26	0.07	0.00	0.40	0.73
GOA	0.15	0.42	0.00	0.14	0.71
ASSAM	2.57	0.65	2.49	1.10	6.81
ARUNACHAL PRADESH	0.18	0.00	0.00	0.05	0.23
MANIPUR	0.18	0.00	0.00	0.23	0.41
MEGHALAYA	0.30	0.00	0.11	0.01	0.42
NAGALAND	0.29	0.13	0.00	0.11	0.53
SIKKIM	0.11	0.00	0.00	0.07	0.18
TRIPURA	0.34	0.24	0.00	0.31	0.89
MIZORAM	0.18	0.00	0.00	0.00	0.18
JHARKHAND	1.23	0.35	0.00	0.35	1.93
UTTRANCHAL	1.68	0.76	0.00	0.00	2.44
CHHATISGARH	10.40	2.09	6.70	0.00	19.19
UNION TERRITORIES	5.41	1.73	0.00	0.00	7.14
GRAND TOTAL	252.96	102.82	199.49	170.60	725.87

* Storage capacity of FCI as on 01-06-2006

** Storage capacity of CWC and SWCs as on 01-06-2006

***This information have been taken from the State Profiles prepared on the basis of the information obtained from various states in 1998-99

This capacity of the FCI includes 84.99 lakh MT capacity hired from the CWC and SWCs.

Apart from the FCI, CWC and SWC the storage capacity also exists in cooperative and private sector. The National Cooperative Development Corporation (NCDC) has been assisting cooperative marketing societies functioning at the mandi, district, regional, state and national levels for construction of godowns of their own to create storage facility, to expand the existing capacity and also for renovation/ up gradation of rural godowns under the Central Sector and Corporation Sponsored Schemes. The National Cooperative Development Corporation was established by an Act of Parliament in 1963 as a statutory Corporation under the Ministry of Agriculture. NCDC also provides financial assistance to Co-operative Marketing Societies and their federations through State Government directly on a selective basis under various schemes. Assistance is provided directly on receipt of guarantee of Central Govt for the societies located in U.Ts.

In our country the small and marginal farmers do not have the economic strength to retain the produce and compelled to sell the produce at a time when the prices are not favorable. It has been absorbed that there is an additional need in the country to provide the farming community with facilities for storage to enhance their holding capacity in order to sell their produce at remunerative prices and avoid distress sales which would also help to meet the credit requirement of farmers as well as to avoid the wastage and produce deterioration. Accordingly, Gramin Bhandaran Yojana, a Capital Investment Subsidy Scheme for Construction / Renovation of Rural Godowns was introduced in 2001-2002 by the Central Goverenment. The scheme is being implemented by Directorate of Marketing and Inspection (DMI), Department of Agriculture and Cooperation Ministry of Agriculture in collaboration with NABARD and NCDC.

The main objective of scheme is to create the Scientific storage capacity with allied facilities in rural areas to meet the requirement of farmers for storing the farm produce and agricultural inputs, grading and standardization, prevention of distress sale, strengthen of agricultural marketing system.. prevention of distress sale immediately after harvest by providing the facility of pledge financing and marketing credit, introduction of a national system of warehouse receipts in respect of agricultural commodities stored in such godowns and to reverse the declining trend of investment in agriculture sector by encouraging private and cooperative sectors to invest in the creation of storage infrastructure in the country.

It is a capital investment subsidy scheme for construction/ renovation/expansion of rural Godowns. The scheme provides credit linked back-ended capital investment subsidy @ 25% of the project cost with a ceiling of Rs. 37.50 lakhs per project. For the projects in North-Eastern states and hilly areas with altitude of more than 1000 m above sea level and SC/ST entrepreneurs, maximum subsidy admissible is Rs 50 lakhs @ 33% of the project cost. The total capacity of storage under this scheme has been generated up to June 2006 is 166.70 lakh tones.

The project for construction of rural godowns is open for individuals, farmers, group of farmers/growers, Partnership/ Proprietary firms, Non-Government Organizations (NGO's), Self Help Groups(SHGs), Companies, Corporations, Co-operatives, Federations, Agricultural Produce Marketing Committees, Marketing Boards and Agro Processing Corporations in the entire country. Assistance for renovation of rural godowns, however, restricted to godowns constructed by cooperatives only.

1.8 APPROACH AND OBJECTIVES OF THE BOOK

India covers one fortieth of global land and occupies second position in Asia after china. In Asia, India has the highest proportion of saline irrigated land. Over the period, ground water tables is going down in most of the regions due to over exploitation of water leading to desertification. The prospects of food grains production in the coming years are not encouraging, and resources available to increase agricultural production like land, water and soil fertility are shrinking, at a time when there is need to feed to millions of hungry people.

Low land distribution and hunger always correlate particularly in those countries in which most of the people depend for their livelihood on the primary activities i.e. agriculture, forestry etc. This is particularly true for Indian context as its nearly two-third of total population lives in villages. The per capita land is going to be decline turning farmers into landless laborers. Besides the increasing pressure on land due to tremendous growth of population, the quality of land is also going to degrade mainly due to consumption of fertilizers in unbalanced ratio against the standard norms of N: P: K consumption ratio of 4:2:1.

The requirement of food is a continuous function of time, but availability of food is of discrete nature. The agrarian economy is structurally different from the industrial economy, because of the principles which govern the size and organization of industry do not operate in agriculture.Depletion of fertility, deterioration of land deposits of sand in the event of inundations and submergence by floods and cyclones, erosion by wind and rain, are extremely damaging factors which changes the characteristic of agriculture.

It is a well established fact that when the resources (especially land) and technology constraints limits the aggregate food production, its negative impact on food security can be seen not only on household or individual level but also on state, regional and national level. Confronted by these problems, there should be a growing interest is to increase the local food production. The recent literature on diversification of Indian agriculture indicates that there has been declaration in the growth of food grains, which may cause serious implications for the food security. In fact the growth of food grains during the 90's has been close to the annual population growth rate which implies stagnant per capita production level.Due to high growth rate of population and nearly stagnant growth rate of pulse production, the negative growth rate in pulses production has also been observed. Sustained growth in agriculture production and productivity is essential to over all stability of economy. The question is whether it would be possible to improve output growth in the agricultural sector in future, or may past trends of growth of food grains give the justification of any optimism in this regard.

Indian population is predominantly vegetarian and in their diets cereals such as rice, wheat and coarse cereals are most common source of calories. Because of their relative cheapness, these are always substituted for the most common expensive food stuffs containing oils and fats. Though cereals contain some amount of vegetable proteins over dependence on them results in deficiency of high quality proteins which are available in pulses, thus pulses production is equally essential in Indian context. In the years to come, higher economic growth as well as sizable population growth will increase the requirement of food grains, and therefore there is need to make special efforts to make available the minimum quantity of food grains to feed the entire population. The recent definitions given by scientists and organizations has emphasized the access to balanced diet and dietary needs by the common people which in reality points out the food requirement. The concept of food requirement differs to the concept of food demand in the sense that food demand mainly depends on purchasing power of people and other multivariate factors like taste, price of substitute, consumer preferences etc. The food requirement is unaffected by all these factors and depends mainly on the energy (calorie) need of the individuals and is constant for a particular age group. The speculative hoarding of food grains, private trade and natural factors may change the structure of food grains supply which may increase the cost and price and consequently the availability of food grains to the lower income groups. As calorie requirements vary across the age groups of population, the traditional method of calculating food requirement based on per capita norm suffers from the problem of averaging and thus may give a value wide of the true food requirement. Hence, as a first step, the present study attempts to estimate the population by different age groups with the help of the population projections at state level which are based on Sample Registration System by the technical group, 1996, Registrar General, India, using 1996 as the base year. Thereafter, the separate food grains requirement on the basis of age groups has been estimated and summed up to project the total food grains requirement. The projected food grains requirement (separately for cereals and pulses) is based on least cost balanced diets recommended by Nutrition Advisory Committee of the Indian Council of Medical Research (ICMR) for the people in Indian context. The food grains requirements were estimated at retail level, which consist of allowance at the physiological level plus tentative allowance of 10 percent made for kitchen and other wastages.

Grain storage is a crucial component of the post-harvest chain and to maintain the food security. Storage infrastructure is necessary to carry the food grains from production period to consumption periods distributed over the full year. The production of particular agricultural commodity is of discrete nature while the consumption is a continuous function of time which makes necessary a balanced system of procurement and storage of food grains to maintain the food security.

In order to comply the above situations, it is necessary to have the future estimates of food grains supply as well as requirement in order to prepare the nation well in advance for the purpose to face the situation in respect of food security (incase of deficit) or to plan better strategy for exports (in case of surplus) with a vision of having proper storage facilities. Keeping in view, the present book is proposed to fulfill the following objectives:

1. To estimate the state wise supply of food grains in the country for the years 2005-06 and 2010-11.
2. To estimate the state wise food grains requirement by the different age groups of population for the year, 2005-06 and 2010-11.
3. To estimate the statewise per capita per day availability of food grains for the year 2005-06 and 2010-11.
4. To estimate the food grains storage requirement of the country for the year 2005-06 and 2010-11.
5. To project the food security scenario in the country for the year 2005-06 and 2010-11.
6. To derive policy and planning implications to enhance the food security level for major states and at national level.

The present study analysis the 17 major states* which accounts more than 97 percent of production (1998-99) and population (1991) to the whole India. The selected states in the study are Andhra Pradesh, Assam, Bihar, Gujarat, Haryana, Himachal Pradesh, Jammu and Kashmir, Karnataka, Kerala, Madhya Pradesh, Maharashtra, Orissa, Punjab, Rajasthan, Tamil Nadu, Uttar Pradesh and West Bengal.

While making the projections, it is assumed in analysis that the past trend will continue in future. The net production estimated in analysis refers to the production available for human consumption and was computed after deducting the 12.5% allowance (for seed, feed and wastage etc.) from the Gross Production. The estimates of food grains production have been obtained in three scenarios i.e. upper (optimistic), expected (normal) and lower (pessimistic) level. The procedure and methods adopted in the estimation of food grains production and requirement is explained in chapter II.

The analysis is restricted to food grains due to its significance in balanced diet. Secondly in Indian context, the trends in per capita supply of food grains is always considered as an indicator of the improvement in food security as our first problem is to reduce hunger rather than to divert themselves for other costly items like egg, meat, vegetables, fruits etc. The Indian population is predominantly vegetarian and their diets, cereals dominate the food expenditure and considered as major source of calories. In our country the food security in the long run will depend partly on slowing population growth in the coming decades. Despite the fact that the India has made a satisfactory achievement in food grains production, it is the population growth rate which nullifies the benefits of production. The increased availability of food is necessary

*The states viz Bihar, Madhya Pradesh and Uttar Pradesh mentioned here are undivided. At present, the mentioned undivided Bihar state also includes Jharkhand, Madhya Pradesh and Uttar Pradesh include Chattishgarh and Uttarakhand respectively.

condition for achieving food security in food deficit countries. The food deficit increases when growth rate of population surpasses the growth rate of food supply (food grains in our context), thus examination of food population relation ship is important as requirement of food is directly proportional to the population growth rate. In this context, the study attempts to carry out the detailed examination of food population relation ship in different major states by carrying out the estimation of the production and requirement of food grains and the same given in chapter III. The chapter IV synthesizes the major states and projects the production of food grains and requirement at the national level. The estimated food grains deficit or surplus along with the per capita availability of food grains in the different major states and storage requirement of food grains at national level is given in this chapter. On the basis of present analysis and selected studies, the chapter V focuses on policy and planning implications as well as discusses the ways and approaches needs to be adopted in major states and at national level to enhance the level of food security.

In present analysis the state wise food security scenario for the two time periods i.e. for 2005-06 and 2010-11 were analyzed on the basis of food grains production-requirement gap and the basic strategy proposed is to aim for self-sufficiency of food grains production in the states. The study considers that the adequacy of foodgrains at national or state level does not guarantee the availability of food grains at household level until and unless distribution in proper and there are no constraints of purchasing power for the poor segment of population as also mentioned in earlier studies.

The study strongly believes that the production of food should be as per the requirement of population based on balanced diet norms as it is the food supply-requirement gap which reflects the real status of food security.

CHAPTER 2

METHODOLOGY

The present study is confined at national level and uses the information of 17 major states which account for more than 97% of total population (1991) and food grains production (1998-99) in India. This chapter briefly explains the methods and procedures used in forecasting of food grains, approaches adopted in estimating food grains requirements and specification of variables and data. It is divided into nine sections. Section 2.1, deals with the regression models. Section 2.2, describes the meaning, characteristics and suitability of regression models. Sections 2.3 and 2.4, explain the methods related to Moving Averages and Exponential Smoothing respectively. Section 2.5 explains criteria to determine the adequacy of forecasting model. Section 2.6 is devoted to explain the prediction interval used in forecasting of food grains. Sections 2.7 and 2.8 explains the conceptual framework for the estimation of food grains requirement and demographic projections by age groups respectively. The specification of variables and data which includes selection of study period, selection of crops and data sources are explained in section 2.9.

2.1 REGRESSION MODELS

The study considers the regression analysis of time series data and other forecasting techniques for making the projections of food grains production. The models considered in regression analysis are Linear, Quadratic, Modified exponential and Exponential. The analysis of forecasting of production assumes that the past trends of production will continue in future.

	Name of Regression model	*Algebraic form*
1.	Linear	$y = a + bt + u_t$
2.	Quadratic	$y = a + bt + ct^2 + u_t$
3.	Modified exponential or quadratic Curve fitted to logarithms	$Y = \alpha + \beta t + \gamma t^2 + u_t$ (where ln y =Y, ln a= α, ln b=β, ln c= γ)
4.	Exponential	$y = ae^{bt}$

where y is dependent variable , 't' is time, 'u'_t is error term and a, b, c etc. are estimated regression coefficients).

In regression models in which time 't' is taken as the trend or independent variable, the interest is to see that how dependent variable behaves over time. The trend variable reflects composite effect of independent variables which influence 'y'. The growth path may be linear or quadratic or any one of other forms. The objective is not to look for the causes behind the upward or downward trends but simply to describe the pattern of data over time.

2.2 MEANING, CHARACTERISTICS AND SUITABILITY OF REGRESSION MODELS

Linear

The value of parameter b>0 in linear function reflects the positive growth in 'y' over time i.e. increasing trend, while b<0 shows the decreasing trend. The value of b=0 means that there is no change in 'y' over time.

Quadratic

A function of the form $y = f(x) = b_1x^n + b_2x^{n-1} + \ldots\ldots\ldots\ldots b2_m x + b_{m+1}$, where n is a positive integer called polynomial of degree 'n'. When the polynomial function is of degree 2 i.e. n=2, then it is called quadratic function. A quadratic curve either falls at first shows the minimum value of y or it rises at first and exhibits the maximum value. In this function, b>0 or 'b' and 'c' with opposite signs make sense in trend analysis.

Exponential function

If the independent variable in any functional relationship appears as an exponent (or power) , then the functional relationship is called exponential function. There are several exponential forms used like, $y=b^t$, $y=ab^t$, $y= ab^{ct}$, $y=ae^t$, $y=ae^{bt}$(where a, b, c and e are constants and $b \neq 1$ as well as taking only positive values).

The form $y=ae^{bt}$ is always used to calculate the Compound Annual Growth Rate (CAGR).

The exponential form can be changed into linear form by taking ln (Log) to apply the OLS techniques

i.e. $\ln y = \ln a + b\, t \ln_e e$ or $\ln y = \alpha + bt$ where, $\ln a = \alpha$

The CAGR in present case is $(e^{b}-1) \times 100$.

Modified exponential or quadratic curve fitted to logarithms

Original form of this function is $y = a\, b^t c^{t2}$

Taking ln (Logorithim) on both sides

$\ln y = \ln a + t \ln b + t^2 \ln c$ ([) or $Y = \alpha + \beta t + \gamma t^2 + u_t$,

where $\ln y = Y$, $\ln a = \alpha$, $\ln b = \beta$, $\ln c = \gamma$

On differentiation, $d(\ln y / dt) = \beta + 2\gamma t$ i.e. the changing growth rate over the time is equal to $\beta + 2\gamma t$.

for positive β, the sign of γ would indicate whether there is acceleration or deceleration in growth. If $\beta > 0, \gamma > 0$ then there is acceleration in growth at the increasing rate and if $\beta > 0, \gamma < 0$ then the curve rises to the maximum and then falls. The turning point is obtained by putting

$d(\ln y / dt) = 0$ (for maxima or minima)

or $\beta + 2\gamma t = 0$ or the turning point is observed at $t = \frac{-\beta}{2\gamma}$

An analysis of time series data extends the historical pattern into the future and is not capable of predicting points in activity level. This is the reason that the regression relationships involving cubes or higher powers of 't' has been avoided in the present analysis. The regression models containing cubes and higher powers of 't' can not be used to forecast the turning point. Secondly, for a fixed amount of data i.e. n, corresponding to more and more regressors, the Durbin Watson lower bound (d_L) values move closer to 0, and the Durbin Watson upper bound (du) values move closer to 2 widening the inconclusive band. So more regressors means a stricter test of hypothesis and a greater chance of its rejection (Hebden, 1983).

2.3 MOVING AVERAGES

Simple Moving Average

The SMA is used with the assumption of a constant pattern and intended for data having no trend. The model for the response in period t is $y_t = \hat{a} + \varepsilon_t$, where ε_t is random variable with mean 0 and variance $ó^2_\varepsilon$ and a is unknown parameter which should be estimated to forecast the future values. If all the data used in analysis is given equal weight and least square criterion is used to estimate "a" then it can be shown that

$$\hat{a} = 1 / N \sum_{t-N+1}^{t} Y_t = M_t$$

at the end of period t, the forecast for period T is just $y_{(t+T)} = M_t$ where M_t(or $M_t^{[1]}$) is called N period moving average.

Double Moving Average

If the data has linear trend and SMA technique is applied then bias is observed which equals (N-1/2)b, where b is the slope of the linear trend. In order to correct this bias, DMA should be calculated. The equation used in forecasting, which uses DMA and able to correct the bias is $y_{t+T} = a_t + b_t.T$

where T is the number of time periods from the present time, to the period to be forecasted and $a_t = 2M_t^{[1]} - M_t^{[2]}$, $b_t = (2 / N-1)(M_t^{[1]} - M_t^{[2]})$, where $M_t^{[1]}$is moving average and $M_t^{[2]}$ refers to the double moving average i.e. an average of the moving averages.

2.4 EXPONENTIAL METHODS

Simple Exponential Smoothing

The model used in SES is

$$Y_t = a + \varepsilon_t$$

Where a is expected production in any period and

ε_t = random component having mean 0 and variance σ^2_ε.

If the available data is $y_1, y_2, \ldots\ldots y_t$, then through the use of this information and by applying the exponential smoothing , the updated estimate â (t) (= $S_t^{[1]}$) can be calculated though the basic exponential smoothing model.

$$S_t^{[1]} = \alpha\, x_t + (1-\alpha)\, S_{t-1}^{[1]}$$

i.e. *new estimate* = α *(new data)* + $(1-\alpha)$ *(previous estimate)* where the term S_t refers to weighted average of all past observations (i.e. and the superscript [1] in S_t is applied for first order exponential smoothing.

In determining $S_1^{[1]}$ in above exponential model , the $S_0^{[1]}$ should be estimated . As the SES fits for data which basically have no trend, an estimate based on the average of the first few data points can be taken as for the value for $S_0^{[1]}$.

Double Exponential Smoothing

The equation used in forecasting which uses DES

$$y_{t+T} = a_t + b_t.T$$

where T is the number of time periods from the present time, to the period to be forecasted and

$$a_t = 2S_t^{[1]} - S_t^{[2]},$$

$$b_t = (\alpha/1-\alpha)\,(S_t^{[1]} - S_t^{[2]}),$$

where $S_t^{[1]}$ is first-order exponential smoothing and $S_t^{[2]}$ refers to the second-order exponential smoothing. These smoothed statistics are developed on the basis of original origin of time. $S_t^{[1]}$ can be developed by

$S_t^{[1]} = \alpha\, x_t + (1-\alpha)\, S_{t-1}^{[1]}$ and $S_t^{[2]}$ by $S_t^{[2]} = \alpha\, S_t^{[1]} + (1-\alpha)\, S_{t-1}^{[2]}$.

Initial values for $S_0^{[1]}$ and $S_0^{[2]}$ can be obtained from estimates of the two coefficients developed from simple regression analysis in following manner.

$S_0^{[1]} = \hat{a}_1 - \beta/\alpha(\hat{a}_2)$ and $S_0^{[2]} = \hat{a}_1 - 2\beta/\alpha(\hat{a}_2)$,where $\hat{a}_1$ and $\hat{a}_2$ are two estimated coefficients at the original origin and $\beta = 1 - \alpha$

In exponential smoothing, the weight given to previous observations decreases geometrically with age and the choice of smoothing constant (α) is important in determining the operating characteristics of exponential smoothing. The smoothing constant in simple exponential smoothing is calculated by the following formula.

$$\alpha = (2 / N+1),$$

where N refers to most recent observations. As a general rule the smoothing constant for a constant model should be between 0.01 and 0.3. The equivalent s moothing constant (α_2) for DES is calculated by,

$$\alpha_2 = 1-(1-\alpha)^{1/2}$$

Triple Exponential Smoothing

The basic n[th] degree polynomial model of the form for the exponential smoothing is

$y_t = b_1 + b_2 t. + (b_3/2!)t_t^2 + \ldots\ldots. + (b_{n+1}/n!)t_t^n + \varepsilon_t$, where ε_t is a random variable having $E(\varepsilon_t)=0$ and $V(\varepsilon_t)= \sigma_\varepsilon^2$ and $y_1, y_2 \ldots\ldots. y_t$ is available data (in the present analysis it implies the data for production).

The forecasting equation at the current origin (i.e. origin defined at the end of period t) used in analysis for Triple Exponential Smoothing is

$$y_{t+T}(t) = \hat{a}_1(t) + \hat{a}_2(t).T + 1/2\ \hat{a}_3(t)T^2$$

where T is the number of time periods forecasted from the present time t and $\hat{a}_1(t)$, $\hat{a}_2(t)$ and $\hat{a}_3(t)$ are the values at current origin which can be estimated as,

$$\hat{a}_1(t)=3S_t^{[1]}-3S_t^{[2]}+S_t^{[3]},$$

$$\hat{a}_2(t)=1/2(\alpha/1-\alpha)^2\,[(6-5\alpha)S_t^{[1]}-2(5-4\alpha)S_t^{[2]}+(4-3\alpha)S_t^{[3]}],$$

$$\hat{a}_3(t)=(\alpha/1-\alpha)^2\,[S_t^{[1]}-2S_t^{[2]}+S_t^{[3]}]$$

where $S_t^{[1]}$ is first-order exponential smoothing, $S_t^{[2]}$ is the second-order exponential smoothing and $S_t^{[3]}$ refers to the triple-order exponential smoothing computed at the end of period t.

$S_t^{[1]}$ can be developed by $S_t^{[1]}=\alpha x_t+(1-\alpha)S_{t-1}^{[1]}$, $S_t^{[2]}$ by $S_t^{[2]}=\alpha S_t^{[1]}+(1-\alpha)S_{t-1}^{[2]}$ and $S_t^{[3]}$ by $S_t^{[3]}=\alpha S_t^{[2]}+(1-\alpha)S_{t-1}^{[3]}$. Starting initial values (i.e. $S_0^{[1]}$, $S_0^{[2]}$ and $S_0^{[3]}$) must be provided for the three smoothed statistics which were obtained from least square estimates of the model coefficients at original origin basis in the following manner,

$$S_0^{[1]}=\hat{a}_1-\beta/\alpha(\hat{a}_2)+\beta(2-\alpha)/2\,\alpha^2(\hat{a}_3)$$

$$S_0^{[2]}=\hat{a}_1-2\beta/\alpha(\hat{a}_2)+2\beta(3-2\alpha)/2\,\alpha^2(\hat{a}_3)$$

$$S_0^{[3]}=\hat{a}_1-3\beta/\alpha(\hat{a}_2)+3\beta(4-3\alpha)/2\,\alpha^2(\hat{a}_3)$$

where $\hat{a}_1$ $\hat{a}_2$ and $\hat{a}_3$ are three estimated coefficients at the original origin and $\beta = 1-\alpha$, αrefers to smoothing constant.

In exponential smoothing, the weight given to previous observations decreases geometrically with age and the choice of smoothing constant (α) is important in determining the operating characteristics of exponential smoothing. The smoothing constant in simple exponential smoothing is calculated by the following formula.

$\alpha = (2/N+1)$, where N refers to most recent observations.

The equivalent smoothing constant (á$_3$) for TES is calculated by

$$\alpha_3 = 1-(1-\alpha)^{1/3}$$

2.5 CRITERIA TO DETERMINE THE ADEQUACY OF FORECASTING MODEL

The main criterion to determine the adequacy of a regression model used in analysis are the significance of estimates of parameters, detection of serial correlation , adjusted R^2 and the sign of the estimated coefficients. A regression model is considered adequate in forecasting when the estimates of parameters in the model are statistically significant which have been tested by applying t-test. F-test has been used to determine statistical confidence about the strength of relationship between the variables. In present analysis, an á value (level of significance) of .05 and .10 is employed, which means that there are 5 and 10% chances of rejecting a statistical hypothesis concerning parameter of interest. When $F_{cal} > F_{\alpha,k-1,n-k}$ then at least one parameter in the model are statistically significant i.e. non zero, on the other hand if $F_{cal} < F_{\alpha,k-1,n-k}$, then all parameters in the model are zero and a very poor regression model has been constructed. If $t_{cal} > t_{\alpha/2,n-k}$,then the parameters is assumed to be non-zero or null hypothesis (H_0) is rejected and alternative hypothesis (H_1) is accepted i.e. $H_1 > \beta \neq 0$ and vice versa. In case of existence of serial correlation, there is underestimation of true variance and the usual test of significance i.e. t and f test are not valid. Therefore, before proceeding for regression analysis to use for projections, the Durbin-Watson (d statistic) was also used to check the serial correlation.

R^2 (or r^2 for one explanatory variable) has been the quick guide that how well particular sample is fitted by the regression hyper plane as well as to compare the regression based models. Some authors de-emphasize the use of R^2 as a measure of goodness of fit as well as use for comparing two or more R^2 values. However, "a high R^2 is not evidence in favour of model and a low R^2 is not evidence against it "(Gold berger,1991). In regression analysis, "the objective is not to obtain a high R^2, but to obtain dependable estimates of the true population regression coefficients and draw statistical inference about them" (Gujrati, 1995). Therefore, the researcher should be more concerned about the statistical significance of explanatory variable to the independent variable. If R^2 is high, well and good, on the other hand if R^2 is low, it does not mean that the model is necessarily bad (Achen,1982, and Gragner and Newbold, 1976). However, it is a matter of fact that the value of R^2 can be raised either by fitting a polynomial of n-1 to the n data point or by selecting the portion of data in order to get a satisfactory fit. In both the cases the model will be worth less predictor (Hebden,1983).

In case if regression techniques was not found suitable then as a second step, we proceeded for other forecasting techniques i.e. Moving averages and Exponential methods as these techniques are able to deal directly with serial correlation in time series data while regression based techniques are not. Moving averages used in forecasting includes Simple Moving Average (SMA) and Double Moving Average (DMA) methods. Exponential smoothing used in forecasting in the present analysis includes Simple Exponential Smoothing (SES), Double Exponential Smoothing (DES), Triple Exponential Smoothing (TES) and exponential smoothing of higher orders. The SMA or SES fits for data which is basically constant and have no trend .The DMA or DES techniques is appropriate for the linear trend while Triple Exponential Smoothing is appropriate for data which shows curvature.

When the regression techniques are not applied and the task is to make the projections through using other forecasting techniques, then the problem comes when there is choice between SMA and SES or DMA and DES . In that case the Mean Square Error (MSE) criterion is used in the study i.e. the Mean Square Error of each technique is compared and the forecasting method, which gives the smallest MSE, is selected,

The choice of technique between SMA and SES or DMA and DES is carried out through the criteria of Mean Square Error (MSE) and the forecasting method, which gives the smallest MSE, has been selected. The MSE is calculated as,

$$MSE = 1/n \sum_{i=1}^{n} (forecast_i - actual_i)^2$$

Since, MSE depends on actual production, the estimates of which are not available, therefore in the present analysis, only for the comparison purposes, an extra exercise was done to make forecast on the basis of first ten years i.e. from 1984-85 to 1993-94 and the forecast of next five years from 1994-95 to 1998-99 were compared to the actual values.

If the results do not look encouraging due to very few coefficients being statistically significant or have the incorrect signs or because the Durbin-Watson statistic is too low or the very low R^2 value than the model needs to be corrected (Hebden,1983).

Often there are cases, when there is little choice to determine the model adequacy between linear or non-linear function. In such cases the linear function must be selected as it is always safe to use the linear function to fit the data the even in worst conditions which is not possible through choosing the non linear functions. Among the non-linear functions a Modified exponential or quadratic curve fitted to logarithms is always preferred over the Quadratic Function. It is always good to estimate exponential function up to four or five points because of its sensitive nature or to get a maximum true value.

A time series takes only time ordered sequence of observations of a variable and its analysis develop a model for predicting future values through the past observations of the variable to be forecasted. In regression based analysis, the equal weight is assigned to all the past observations and a forecaster should try to select that portion of data which represent the true segment of past observations i.e. the past observations selected should not be over dominant. Similar case happens also in the methods based on averages as these methods also assume that the past trend will continue in future. But, the results might be less affected in exponential methods as in exponential smoothing, the weight given to previous observations decreases geometrically with age of data and the choice of smoothing constant (α) is important in determining the operating characteristics.

Even after taking all the precautions, the forecasted results might be not true and its accuracy decreases as planning time increases. Also there may be a random variation in the process and unexpected errors in estimating the parameter in the model. Therefore, it is always good to determine the prediction interval at some probability level in which the estimated forecast may vary. It is also added that, the techniques used in the present analysis is suitable only for short term projections.

In brief, the following techniques were used in the projection of cereals and pulses for the different major states.

Table 2.1: Selected projection techniques for the projection of cereals and pulses for the different major states.

S.No.	State	Selected projection technique for cercals	Selected projection technique for pulses
1.	Andhra Pradesh	Regression	Triple Exponential Smoothing
2.	Assam	Regression	Triple Exponential Smoothing
3.	Bihar	Regression	Triple Exponential Smoothing
4.	Gujrat	Regression	Regression
5.	Haryana	Double Moving Average	Simple Moving Average
6.	Himachal Pradesh	Double Exponential Smoothing	Regression
7.	Jammu and Kashmir	Regression	Regression
8.	Karnataka*	Regression	Regression
9.	Kerala	Double Exponential Smoothing	Simple Exponential Smoothing
10.	Madhya Pradesh	Regression	Regression
11.	Maharashtra	Regression	Regression
12.	Orissa	Regression	Simple Moving Average
13.	Punjab	Regression	Regression
14.	Rajasthan	Double Moving Average	Regression
15.	Tamil Nadu	Regression	Simple Exponential Smoothing
16.	Uttar Pradesh	Regression	Regression
17.	West Bengal	Regression	Regression

*In Karnataka state, the regression technique was also found suitable for production trends of pulses, but the statistical evidence (through D-W statistic) concluded that the results of serial correlation are inconclusive for the pulses production in the state. Hence, the model has been corrected in this case through the transformed variable data and the new transformed model having minimum variance estimates has been estimated through OLS.

2.6 PREDICTION INTERVAL IN FORECASTING

Forecasting gives a prediction about future events with the assumption that the process will behave in future as it did it in the recent past and the model form used in forecasting is correct and that the true parameters do not change. In most situations these assumptions are not correct and the underlying process changes with time, which makes forecasting accuracy to decrease as the planning lead time increases. The accuracy is described by the variance of the forecast error. Even if the forecast error does not change over time, the forecast will differ from the actual variable because of the random variation in the process and errors in estimating the parameter in the model. Thus, the variance of forecast error is a function of the variance of the process and the sampling variances of the statistics used to estimate model parameters. Adding and subtracting a multiple of standard de*via*tion of forecast error can convert the point estimate converted into prediction interval that may describe an uncertainty associated with a forecast. In the present analysis, the 95 % prediction interval for the periods has been determined and the forecasting interval at the probability level of 0.95 is $y_{t+T} \pm 1.96\,\sigma_{et}$ i.e. our forecast in 95% cases may vary between $y_{t+T} + 1.96\sigma_{et}$ (upper range level) and $y_{t+T} - 1.96\sigma_{et}$ (lower range level) and the expected value is the average of these two estimated values. The methods of determination of confidence interval are different for different approaches. An estimate of the standard de*via*tion of the forecasting error σ_{et}^2 is necessary to compute the forecasting interval which is a function of σ_ε^2 i.e. variance in production process of which the estimation is very difficult. (Brown, 1962) reports a study involving relationship between the standard de*via*tion of forecast error, $\sigma_{e,}$ and the average demand rate a (process variable) was found i.e. $\sigma_e = 0.82a^{0.75}$.The same is equivalent to

$$\Delta=0.66a^{0.75} \text{ by using, } \Delta= 2\int_{\mu}^{\infty} (e-\mu)(2\pi\sigma_e^2)^{-1/2} \exp.(^{e-\mu}/\sigma_e)^2 de \approx 0.8\ \sigma_e$$

assuming forecast error is normally distributed with mean μ and variance σ_e^2 (Johnson and Montagomary, 1976). These relationships help to determine the prediction interval in forecasting methods other than regression techniques.

In regression techniques the mean square about regression s^2 will provide an estimate, based on (n-2) degrees of freedom, of the variance about the regression which would represent a measure of the error for the predicted mean value of y for a given X_k on the transformed scale. The 95 % confidence limits for the true mean value of y for a given X_k are given by,

$$y \pm t\ (n-2\ ,\ 1-\alpha/2)\ (\text{est. se } y_k)$$

Over all the estimation of σ_{et}^2 (or s^2 in regression analysis) helps to observe the uncertainty in production and higher value of the σ_{et}^2 means that the gap between upper and lower level is high and vice versa.

The result of projection is obtained in three different scenaries i.e. lower (pessimistic), expected (normal) and upper (optimistic) level. The net production refers to the production available for human consumption and was computed after deducting 12.5% allowance for seed, feed and wastages. The total seed, feed and wastages have been assumed as 12.5% of the gross but put comprising of 5% towards seed, 5% towards feed and 2.5% towards wastage (GOI, 2001).

2.7 CONCEPTUAL FRAMEWORK FOR THE ESTIMATION OF FOOD GRAINS REQUIREMENT

As calorie requirements vary across the age groups of population, the traditional method of calculating food requirement based on per capita norm suffers from the problem of averaging and thus may give a value wide of the true food requirement. Hence, as a first step, the present study attempts to estimate the population by different age groups with the help of the population projections at state level. Thereafter, the separate food grains requirement on the basis of age groups has been estimated and summed up to project the total food grains requirement. The projected food grains requirement (separately for cereals and pulses) is based on least cost balanced diets recommended by Nutrition Advisory Committee of the Indian Council of Medical Research (ICMR) for the people in Indian context. The food grains requirements were estimated at retail level, which consist of allowance at the physiological level plus tentative allowance of 10% made for kitchen and other wastages. The estimation of food grains requirement for a particular age group depends on the per capita requirement at retail level of that age group and its corresponding population.

To convert per capita food grains requirement at retail level by the physiological level, a tentative allowance of 10% is made for kitchen and other wastages (ICMR, 1984).

The per capita requirement at retail level for a specific age group

= Per capita requirement for specific age group at physiological level x 1.1

The requirement (S_{ij}) either for cereals or pulses for the particular i[th] age group of the jth state for a year is,

$S_{ij} = r_{ik} G_{ijt} \times 365$ where, i =1, 2, 3.... n (age groups) and j =1, 2, 3.... m (states) and,

r_{ik} refers to per day per capita requirement of kth food group (cereals or pulses) for i[th] age group, G_{ijt} refers to the population of ith age group for j[th] state at time t . Summation of S_{ij} gives the total requirement at state level for all the age groups i.e. the total requirement (R) either for cereals or pulses for a year for any state at time t is,

$$R_t = \sum_{i=1}^{n} S_{ij}$$ here 'j' refers for the particular state and 't' refers for the projection years i.e. 2006 or 2011.

As per ICMR norms the per day balanced diet requirement by age groups for different foodstuffs is given for 1-3 years, 4-6 years, 10-12 years (boys), 10-12 years (girls), adults (men) and adults (women).

The food requirement for the age group 7-9 years has been calculated on the basis of average calorie requirement of 4-7 years (children), 10-12 years (boys) and 10-12 years (girls). The diet requirements for adult males and females being taken as that needed for moderate work requirement, rather than a weighted average of sedentary, heavy and moderate work as adequate data is not available for calculating relevant weights. The forecasted requirement at retail level is corrected upto two decimal points.

2.8 APPROACH FOR DEMOGRAPHIC PROJECTIONS BY AGE GROUPS

The estimation of food grains requirement requires the corresponding population figures for the groups, which were estimated, as on 1st March, with the help of projections based on Sample Registration System by the technical group, 1996, Registrar General, India and required data on population collected from the census reports. In order to construct the population, the Compound Annual Growth Rate (CAGR) was calculated between 1991 to 1996, 1996 to 2001, 2001 to 2006 and 2006 to 2011. On the basis of this CAGR, the total population figures for the year from 1991 to 2011, as on 1st March, was constructed which helped out to estimate the population figures by age groups.

Let P_1, P2,........P_{21} refers to the total population as on 1st March, for the year 1991, 1992,.......2011 respectively and X_0, X_1, X_2 .....refers to the population for 0 year*, 1 year, 2 years etc.

Then age wise population distribution as on 1st March for the year 2006 is $X_0=P_{16}-P_{15}$, $X_1=P_{15}-P_{14}$, $X_2=P_{14}-P_{13}$........and so on and similarly for the year 2011 is $X_0=P_{21}-P_{20}$, $X_1=P_{20}-P_{19}$ and $X_2=P_{19}-P_{18}$ etc.

If G_1, G_2, G_3 and G_4 refers to the population of 1-3 years, 4-6 years, 7-9 years and 10-12 years respectively then,

$$G_1=\sum_{i=1}^{3} X_i,\ G_2=\sum_{i=4}^{6} X_i,\ G_3=\sum_{i=7}^{9} X_i \text{ and } G_4=\sum_{i=10}^{12} X_i$$

and remaining population is, $G_R = G_T - [\sum_{i=1}^{4} G_i + G_0]$

where G_T refers to the total population and here G_0 (population of age of zero years) = X_0

Separate population of male and female has been determined on the basis of latest sex ratio available and it is assumed that it is same for the projection years. The approach for demographic estimations also assumes that there is no inter state migration during the period of analysis.

2.9 APPROACH FOR THE ESTIMATION OF FOOD GRAINS STORAGE

The storage requirement is directly proportional to Marketed Surplus and production. The Marketed Surplus is estimated by multiplying Marketed Surplus Ratio (MSR) to the

*The population of zero years refers to those children with an age of less than 365 days.

estimates of Quantity of Production of agricultural commodities. The Marketed surplus therefore equals to

Marketed Surplus = MSR × Quantity of Production

In practice MSRs are always worked out on the basis of production value of three years average production to remove the bias on account of fluctuation in individual commodity and over all production. The estimates of MSR (i.e. 59.6 for food grains) taken in the present exercise is based on the surveys by Government.

The estimated storage requirement, in the present exercise, is based on seasonal and distribution approach. The kharif food grain dominates the overall food grains production i.e. about 52 to 58% (average 54%) of total production. It means the storage requirement is roughly about 54% of total marketed surplus which can also maintain Rabi production *via* assuming that the produce normally stays for the 6 months, and the storage would be capable to maintain the rest of the production of rabi crop .

2.10 SPECIFICATION OF VARIABLES AND DATA

The forecasting in the present study uses the time series data of food grains productions (cereals and pulses separately) from 1984-85 to 1998-99 in which the year 1984-85 reveals the base period. The analysis is restricted for the food grain crops, which include cereals and pulses, and our focus has been to deal separately with these groups rather than their aggregates because of recognized role of pulses or legume crops in the area of nutritional balance in the human diet.

The cereals and pulses includes the following crops :

(i) **Cereals:** Rice, Wheat, Jowar, Bajra , Maize ,Ragi, Barley, and small millets.

(ii) **Pulses:** Gram, Tur and other pulses.

An attempt has been made to embody the latest available data on related economic variables at the time of analysis The study is exclusively based on the secondary data obtained from the various issues of Economic Surveys (Ministry of Finance), Indian Agriculture in Brief (Directorate of Economics and Statistics, Ministry of Agriculture). The data on population has been collected from the census of population (different series). Population projections at state level which are based on Sample Registration System by the technical group, 1996, Registrar General, India, using 1996 as the base year, is collected from Statistical Out line of India 1999-2000, Tata Services Limited, Department of Economics and Statistics, Bombay House. The data on balanced diet for various groups is based on the recommendations of dietary allowances prepared by the Indian Council of Medical Research.

Chapter 3

FOOD GRAINS SUPPLY AND REQUIREMENT: PROJECTIONS FOR MAJOR STATES

There are year to year variation in area under cultivation under crops and yield per hectare which determines the total output. The regional pattern of the growth of output is determined by the number of factors or combination of physical features like fertility of soil, weather, rainfall etc. in coordination with the available technology, level of inputs and irrigation facilities and consumption pattern of local people.

The supply of food grains, which is always considered as an improvement in food security, comprises two crop groups, namely cereals and pulses. The major states selected in the present study accounts approximately 97% of total population (1991) and food grains production (1998-99) in India. The trends during the period from 1984-85 to 1998-99 are analyzed to forecast the production for the years 2005-06 and 2010-11 which is about to close the Tenth and Eleventh Five Year Plan. It is a well established fact that no forecasting system can generate the perfect forecast therefore the results of projection has been explained in three scenarios i.e. lower (pessimistic), expected (normal) and upper (optimistic) level. In the present analysis, the 95% prediction interval for the periods has been determined i.e. our forecast in 95% cases may vary between upper range level and lower range level and the expected value is the average of these two estimated values. The methods of determination of confidence interval are different for different approaches as explained in our methodology chapter.

The projection of food grains requirement, separately for cereals and pulses, depends on the projected population of different age groups and the balanced diet requirements for cereals and pulses recommended by ICMR. As a matter of fact, the calorie requirement vary among individuals, and therefore the per capita requirement on aggregate bases cannot be applied to all the age group of population, and due to this reason projections obtained on the aggregate base is not close to reality. Therefore, attempts has been made to calculate the agewise food grains requirement and then it has been summed up to obtain the total food grains requirement for the purpose to make the projections true. The food grains requirements were estimated at retail level, which consist of allowance at the physiological level plus tentative allowance of 10% made for kitchen and other wastages. It is assumed in analysis that the food grains requirement for human consumption will increase in same manner as that for non-human consumption.

Keeping in view of objectives, the present study utilize the information of 17 major states *viz.* Andhra Pradesh, Assam, Bihar, Gujarat, Haryana, Himachal Pradesh, Jammu and Kashmir, Karnataka, Kerala, Madhya Pradesh, Maharashtra, Orissa, Punjab, Rajasthan, Tamil Nadu, Uttar Pradesh and West Bengal. Accordingly, the chapter has been divided into 17 sections to cover all major states. The analysis for every state is presented through a particular section which again is divided into 4 sub-sections. Besides, a brief introduction in starting is also given to know the location, physical features and general informations of every state. The sub-section I deals with the projection of food grains, separately for cereals and pulses, at pessimistic (lower range), expected and optimistic (upper range) levels. The projection of food grains requirement requires the corresponding population figures (except the age group of zero year) for the different age groups, which were estimated as on 1st March, for the year 2006 and 2011 for every state and the same is given in sub-section II. The sub-section III deals with the food-population relationships and is devoted to present the projection of food grains requirement by population age groups. The sub-section -IV attempts to visualizes the food-security scenario of the state *via* estimating deficit or surplus gap of food grains and per capita per day availability of food grains (excluding 0 years population age group) at pessimistic (lower range), expected and optimistic (upper range) levels.

3.1
ANDHRA PRADESH

The state of Andhra Pradesh has total geographical area of about 27, 676 thousand hectares with population of the state, as per census 2001, is 76, 210, 007 out of which about 27.3% of population resides in urban area. The sex ratio (i.e. females per thousand males) and population density (average number of persons per sq km) is 978 and 277 respectively. The total literacy rate in state is 60.5% which comprises 70.3% for male as against 50.4% for females. The state is bounded on the north by Orissa and Madhya Pradesh, west by Maharashtra and Karnataka, south by Tamil Nadu and on the east by Bay of Bengal.

An approximately 70% population of the state is engaged in agriculture. The major crops in the state are Rice, Groundnut, Sunflower and Cotton. Other important crops are Jowar, Bajra, Maize, Ragi, Tobacco, etc. The state enjoys a position of pre-eminence in respect of crop production particularly food grains and has the distinction of being called the "Rice Bowl" of South India. Rice is a major food crop contributes about 80% of food grains production. Andhra Pradesh is crossed by several rivers, most important are the Godavari and Krishna. The alluvial soils laid down by these rivers are highly fertile and have made Andhra Pradesh one of India's leading agricultural areas. The state has a tropical climate with moderate diffusion to subtropical weather. Humid to semi-humid conditions prevail in the coastal area while arid to semi-arid situations pronounce in the interior parts of the state, particularly Rayalaseema and some districts of Telangana.

3.1.1 PROJECTIONS OF FOOD GRAINS PRODUCTION

The projections of food grains separately for the cereals and pulses for the state of Andhra Pradesh at lower (pessimistic), expected (normal) and upper (optimistic) level for the year 2005-06 and 2010-11 is presented in the Table 3.1.

Table 3.1: Forecasted production of cereals and pulses for the year 2005-06 and 2010-11

(in thousand tonnes)

Crop groups	*Cereals*		*Pulses*	
Year/Production	*2005-06*	*2010-11*	*2005-06*	*2010-11*
Forecasted gross production	14275.05	15733.78	814.78	873.66
95% forecasted gross production prediction interval	14275.05± 2127.77	15733.78 ± 2829.95	814.78± 181.30	873.66± 233.42

Forecasted net production				
Lower range level	10628.87	11290.85	554.29	560.21
Expected range level	12490.66	13767.05	712.93	764.45
Upper range level	14352.46	16243.26	871.57	968.69

The scrutiny of Table 3.1 reveals that the production of food grains in 2005-06 at lower range level will be 11183.16 thousand tonnes with break up of 10628.87 thousand tonnes for cereals and 554.29 thousand tonnes for the pulses. By the year 2010-11, the production will be 11851.06 thousand tonnes with the break up of 11290.85 thousand tonnes for cereals and 560.21 thousand tonnes for pulses.

At upper range level, the production of food grains in 2005-06 will be 15224.03 thousand tonnes with break up of 14352.46 thousand tonnes for cereals and 871.57 thousand tonnes for pulses. By the year 2010-11, the production will be 17211.95 thousand tonnes with the break up of 16243.26 thousand tonnes for cereals and 968.69 thousand tonnes for pulses.

The forecast of the production food grains production in Andhra Pradesh at the expected range level in the year 2005-06 is 13203.59 thousand tonnes which will further grow to 14531.50 thousand tonnes in 2010-11. The production of cereals increased from 12490.66 thousand tonnes in 2005-06 to 13767.05 thousand tonnes in 2010-11. The production of pulses in 2005-06 is 712.93 thousand tonnes which further increased to 764.45 in 2010-11.

3.1.2 ESTIMATES OF POPULATION DISTRIBUTION BY AGE GROUPS

The projection of food grains requirement requires the corresponding population figures (except the age group of zero year) for the different age groups, which were estimated as on 1st March, for the year 2006 and 2011. The estimated population distribution for the state of Andhra Pradesh by different age groups required for the projection of food grains requirement for the two time periods is shown in Fig. 3.1 and 3. 2.

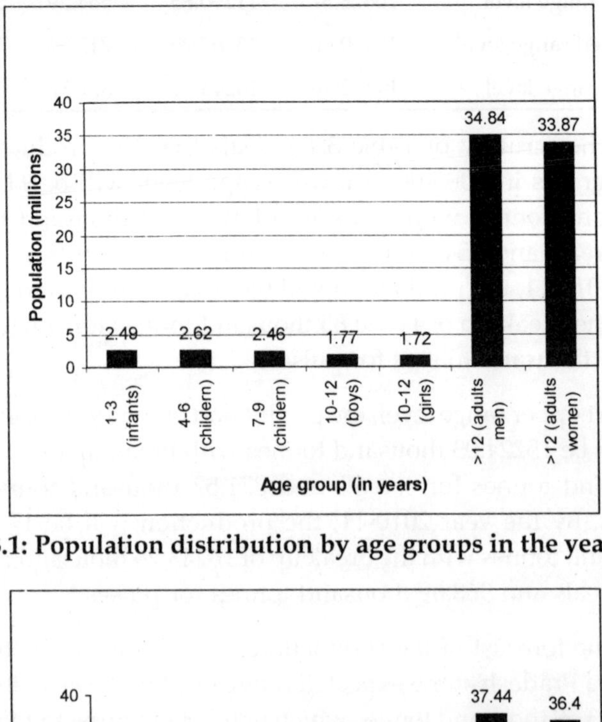

Fig. 3.1: Population distribution by age groups in the year 2006

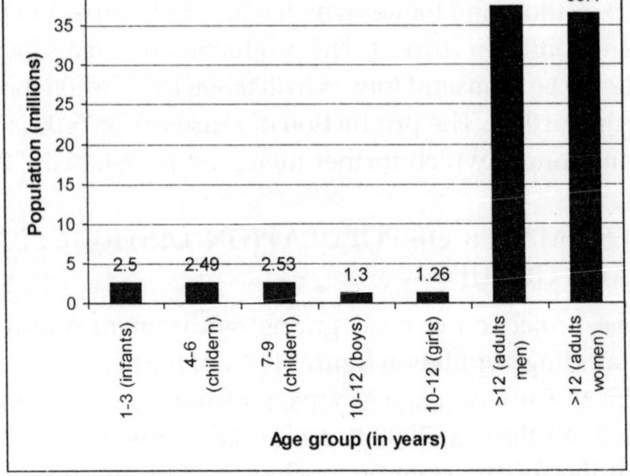

Fig. 3.2: Population distribution by age groups in the year 2011

3.1.3 PROJECTIONS OF FOOD GRAINS REQUIREMENT

The projections for food grain requirement by different age groups separately for cereals and pulses, on the basis of balanced diet has been estimated for the year 2006 and 2011 and the same is given in Table 3.2. On the basis of constructed population distribution by age groups and balanced diet recommendation for cereals and pulses, the estimated results show that the food grains requirement for the Andhra Pradesh state will be 16095.60 and 17018.29 thousand tonnes for the year 2006 and 2011 respectively.The break up will be 14609.86 and 15452.02 thousand tonnes for the cereals and 1485.74 and 1566.27 thousand tonnes of pulses for the two time periods. The requirement for food grains in 2006 by different age groups will be highest in adults (men) i.e. 7969.19 thousand tonnes followed by 6595.37 thousand tonnes for adults (women), 376.31 thousand tonnes for 7-9 years (children), 330.44 thousand tonnes for 10-12 years (boys), 320.84 thousand tonnes for 4-6 years (children), 293.50 thousand tonnes for 10-12 years (girls) and 209.95 thousand tonnes for 1-3 years (infants). By the year 2011, the food grains requirement will be highest in adults (men) i.e. 8568.15 thousand tonnes followed by 7088.14 thousand tonnes for adults (women), 387.01 thousand tonnes for 7-9 years (children), 304.92 thousand tonnes for 4-6 years (children), 243.25 thousand tonnes for 10-12 years (boys), 216.04 thousand tonnes for 10-12 years (girls) and 210.78 thousand tonnes for 1-3 years (infants).

Table 3.2. Forecasted requirement* for cereals and pulses by age groups in 2006 and 2011

(in thousand tonnes)

Food groups	*Cereals*		*Pulses*	
Year /Age groups	*2006*	*2011*	*2006*	*2011*
1-3 years	174.96 (159.05)	175.65 (159.68)	34.99 (31.81)	35.13 (31.93)
4-6 years	284.02 (258.20)	269.93 (245.39)	36.82 (33.47)	34.99 (31.81)

7-9 years		336.80 (306.18)	346.38 (314.89)	39.51 (35.92)	40.63 (36.93)
10-12 years	Boys	298.47 (271.34)	219.76 (199.78)	31.97 (29.03)	23.49 (21.35)
	Girls	262.42 (238.56)	193.27 (175.70)	31.08 (28.25)	22.77 (20.70)
Adults	Men	7269.72 (6608.83)	7816.54 (7105.94)	699.47 (683.28)	751.61 (635.88)
	Women	5983.47 (5439.51)	6430.49 (5845.90)	611.90 (556.27)	657.65 (597.86)
Total		14609.86 (13281.69)	15452.02 (14047.29)	1485.74 (1423.88)	1566.27 (1350.67)

*Forecasted requirement is at retail level.
Figure in parenthesis indicates the forecasted requirement at physiological level.

3.1.4 CONCLUSION

The estimates of food grains production and requirement indicated that overall cereals and pulses requirement would continue to be in deficit condition in both the periods. The net deficit of cereals in the state would be 2119.20 and 1684.97 thousand tonnes in 2005-06 and 2010-11 and 772.81 and 801.82 thousand tonnes for pulses in the same periods. The estimated per capita per day availability (excluding 0 years population age group)# of cereals would be 428.99 and 449.45 grams for the year 2005-06 and 2010-11 while the per capita per day availability of pulses is 24.48 and 24.96 for the same time periods. The estimated ranges i.e. pessimistic range and optimistic range in which the per capita per day availability for cereals may vary is 365.05 to 492.94 grams and 368.61 to 530.29 grams for the year 2005-06 and 2010-11. The estimated limits for the pulses is 19.04 to 29.93 grams and 18.29 to 31.62 grams for the same periods.

The zero year population age group is not considered in estimation of per capita availability of food grains because of their non-significant role in the consumption of the food grains.

3.2
ASSAM

The state of Assam has total geographical area of about 7853 thousand hectares with population of the state, as per census 2001, is 26,655,528 out of which about 12.9% of population resides in urban area. The sex ratio (i.e. females per thousand males) and population density (average number of persons per sq km) is 935 and 340 respectively. The total literacy rate in state is 63.3% which comprises 71.3% for male as against 54.6% for females. The state of Assâm is surrounded by predominantly hilly or mountainous tracts -Bhutan and Arunachal pradesh on the on the north, Manipur, Nagaland and Arunachal Pradesh on the east and Meghalaya, Mizoram and Tripura on the south.

Agriculture accounts for the the livelihood of about four-fifth of the state population and the principal food crop is rice. Of agro-based industries the tea occupies a pivotal place and it is a big industry earning a substantial revenue. Besides tea, which is a plantation crop, the only commercial crop of importance for farmers is jute and mesta. The climate of the state is of the humid tropical type in the plains and subalpine in the hills.

3.2.1 PROJECTIONS OF FOOD GRAINS PRODUCTION

The projections of food grains separately for the cereals and pulses for the state of Assam at lower (pessimistic), expected (normal) and upper (optimistic) level for the year 2005-06 and 2010-11 is presented in the Table 3.3.

Table 3.3: Forecasted production of cereals and pulses for the year 2005-06 and 2010-11

(in thousand tonnes)

Crop groups		*Cereals*		*Pulses*	
Year/Production		***2005-06***	***2010-11***	***2005-06***	***2010-11***
Forecasted gross production		4133.81	4484.31	76.96	87.42
95% forecasted gross production prediction interval		4133.81 ± 109.01	4484.31 ± 145.01	76.96± 13.05	87.42± 36.24
Forecasted net production	Lower range level	3521.70	3796.88	55.92	44.78
	Expected range level	3617.08	3923.77	67.34	76.49
	Upper range level	3712.46	4050.65	78.75	108.20

The scrutiny of Table 3.3 reveals that the production of food grains in 2005-06 at lower range level will be 3577.62 thousand tonnes with break up of 3521.70 thousand tonnes for cereals and 55.92 thousand tonnes for the pulses. By the year 2010-11, the production will be 3841.66 thousand tonnes with the break up of 3796.88 thousand tonnes for cereals and 44.78 thousand tonnes for pulses.

At upper range level, the production of food grains in 2005-06 will be 3791.21 thousand tonnes with break up of 3712.46 thousand tonnes for cereals and 78.75 thousand tonnes for pulses. By the year 2010-11, the production will be 4158.85 thousand tonnes with the break up of 4050.65 thousand tonnes for cereals and 108.20 thousand tonnes for pulses.

The forecast of the food grains production in Assam at the expected range level in 2005-06 will be 3684.42 thousand tonnes which will further grow to 4000.26 thousand tonnes in 2010-11.There will be a phenomenal growth in the state in the production of cereals from 3617.08 thousand tonnes in 2005-06 to 3923.77 thousand tonnes in 2010-11. The production of pulses in 2005-06 is 67.34 thousand tonnes which further increased to 76.49 thousand tonnes in 2010-11.

3.2.2 ESTIMATES OF POPULATION DISTRIBUTION BY AGE GROUPS

The estimated population distribution for the state of Assam by different age groups required for the projection of food grains requirement for the year 2006 and 2011is shown in Fig. 3.3 and 3.4.

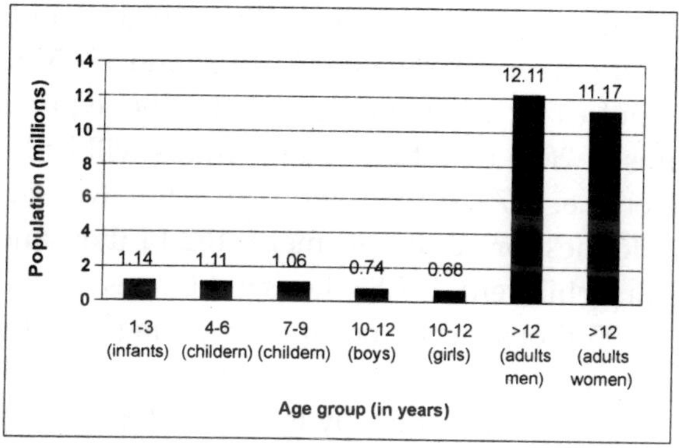

Fig. 3.3: Population distribution by age groups in 2006

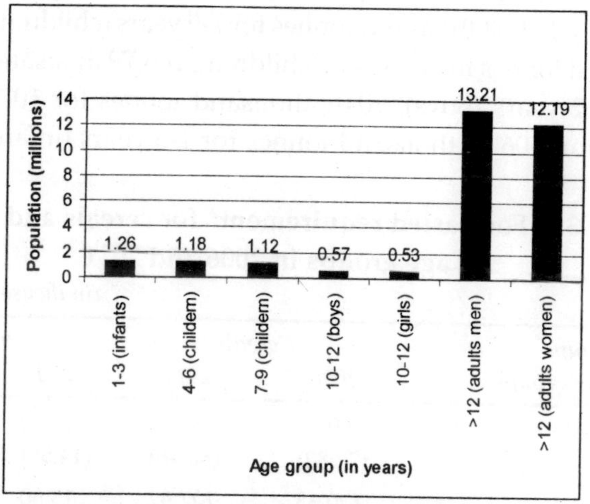

Fig. 3.4: Population distribution by age groups in 2011

3.2.3 PROJECTIONS OF FOOD GRAINS REQUIREMENT

The projections for food grain requirement by different age groups separately for cereals and pulses, on the basis of balanced diet has been estimated for the year 2006 and 2011 and the same is given in Table 3.4. On the basis of constructed population distribution by age groups and balanced diet recommendation for cereals and pulses, the estimated results show that the food grains requirement for the Assam state will be 5594.75 and 6015.79 thousand tonnes for the year 2006 and 2011 respectively. The break up will be 5075.55 and 5458.21 thousand tonnes for the cereals and 519.21 and 557.58 thousand tonnes of pulses for the two time periods. The requirement for food grains in 2006 by different age groups will be highest in adults (men) i.e. 2770.54 thousand tonnes followed by 2175.86 thousand tonnes for adults (women), 162.14 thousand tonnes for 7-9 years (children), 137.86 thousand tonnes for 10-12 years (boys), 135.93 thousand tonnes for 4-6 years (children),116.30 thousand tonnes for 10-12 years (girls) and 96.12 thousand tonnes for 1-3 years (infants). By the year 2011, the food grains requirement will be highest in adults (men) i.e. 3022.83 thousand tonnes followed by 2374.01 thousand tonnes for adults (women), 171.33 thousand tonnes for 7-9 years (children), 144.50 thousand tonnes for 4-6 years (children), 106.79 thousand tonnes for 10-12 years (boys), 90.09 thousand tonnes for 10-12 years (girls) and 106.24 thousand tonnes for 1-3 years (infants).

Table 3.4. Forecasted requirement* for cereals and pulses by age groups in 2006 and 2011

(in thousand tonnes)

Food groups	*Cereals*		*Pulses*	
Year /Age groups	*2006*	*2011*	*2006*	*2011*
1-3 years	80.10 (72.82)	88.53 (80.48)	16.02 (14.56)	17.71 (16.10)
4-6 years	120.33 (109.39)	127.92 (116.29)	15.60 (14.18)	16.58 (15.07)

7-9 years		145.12 (131.93)	153.34 (139.40)	17.02 (15.47)	17.99 (16.35)
10-12 years	Boys	124.52 (113.20)	96.46 (87.69)	13.34 (12.13)	10.33 (9.39)
	Girls	103.99 (94.54)	80.55 (73.23)	12.31 (11.19)	9.54 (8.67)
Adults	Men	2527.51 (2297.74)	2757.67 (2506.97)	243.03 (220.94)	265.16 (241.05)
	Women	1973.98 (1794.52)	2153.74 (1957.94)	201.88 (183.53)	220.27 (200.24)
Total		5075.55 (4614.14)	5458.2 (4962.00)	519.20 (472.00)	557.58 (506.87)

*Forecasted requirement is at retail level.
Figure in parenthesis indicates the forecasted requirement at physiological level.

3.2.4 CONCLUSION

The estimates of food grains production and requirement indicated that overall cereals and pulses requirement would continue to be in deficit condition in both the periods. The net deficit of cereals and pulses in the state would be 1458.47 and 451.87 thousand tonnes in 2005-06 and 1534.44 and 481.09 thousand tonnes in 2010-11.

The estimated per capita per day availability (excluding 0 years population age group) of cereals would be 353.79 and 357.62 grams for the year 2005-06 and 2010-11 while the per capita per day availability of pulses is 6.58 and 6.97 grams for the same time periods. The estimated ranges i.e. pessimistic range and optimistic range in which the per capita per day availability for cereals may vary is 344.46 to 363.12 grams and 346.05 to 369.18 grams for the year 2005-06 and 2010-11. The estimated limits for the pulses is 5.47 to 7.70 grams and 4.08 to [illegible].86 grams for the same periods.

3.3
BIHAR

(The analysis in this section is pertaining to Undivided Bihar)

The Bihar is one of the major states of the Indian Union. On the 15th November, 2000, the new state of Jharkhand was carved out of Bihar as 28th state of India. Now, after the formation of Jharkhand, the Bihar has total geographical area of about 9416 thousand hectares with population of the state, as per census 2001, is 82,998,509 out of which about 10.50% of population resides in urban area. The sex ratio (i.e. females per thousand males) and population density (average number of persons per sq km) is 919 and 881 respectively. The total literacy rate in state is 47.0% which comprises 59.7% for male as against 33.1% for females. The state of Bihar is located in north India. It is bounded in north by Nepal, in east by West Bengal, in west by Uttar Pradesh and in south by Orissa and Jharkhand.The state is suited for agriculture. The important food grain crops are Maize, Paddy, Wheat and Pulses. Main cash crops are sugarcane, potato, tobacco, oilseeds, onion, chilles, jute and mesta. The Bihar is one of the major states of Indian Union. About 89.50 of Bihar's population resides in the villages and Agricultural Economy in Bihar is characterized by predominance of food crops and the existence of large number of small and marginal farmers. The agriculture sector provides livelihood for over 80% of its people and also contributes approx 47% to the state domestic product. There is a need for development in agriculture sector for all round economic development in Bihar as this sector also provides the raw material to the small/village industry.

The newly formed Jharkhand state has total geographical area of about 7971 thousand hectares with population of the state, as per census 2001, is 26,945,829 out of which about 22.20% of population resides in urban area. The sex ratio (i.e. females per thousand males) and population density (average number of persons per sq km) is 941 and 338 respectively. The total literacy rate in state is 53.6% which comprises 67.3% for male as against 38.9% for females. Principle food grain crops are paddy, wheat, maize and pulses.

3.3.1 PROJECTIONS OF FOOD GRAINS PRODUCTION

The projections of food grains separately for the cereals and pulses for the state of Bihar at lower (pessimistic), expected (normal) and upper (optimistic) level for the year 2005-06 and 2010-11 is presented in the Table 3.5.

Table 3.5: Forecasted production of cereals and pulses for the year 2005-06 and 2010-11.

(in thousand tonnes)

Food groups		*Cereals*		*Pulses*	
Year/Age Groups		*2005-06*	*2010-11*	*2005-06*	*2010-11*
Forecasted gross production		14746.25	16057.80	584.81	516.88
95% forecasted gross production prediction interval		14746.25 ± 592.89	16057.80 ±788.55	584.81± 131.92	516.88± 204.09
Forecasted net production	Lower range level	12384.19	13360.59	396.28	273.69
	Expected range level	12902.97	14050.57	511.71	452.27
	Upper range level	13421.74	14740.55	627.14	630.85

The scrutiny of Table 3.5 reveals that the production of food grains in 2005-06 at lower range level will be 12780.47 thousand tonnes with break up of 12384.19 thousand tonnes for cereals and 396.28 thousand tonnes for the pulses. By the year 2010-11, the production will be 13634.28 thousand tonnes with the break up of 13360.59 thousand tonnes for cereals and 273.69 thousand tonnes for pulses.

At upper range level, the production of food grains in 2005-06 will be 14048.88 thousand tonnes with break up of 13421.74 thousand tonnes for cereals and 627.14 thousand tonnes for pulses. By the year 2010-11, the production will be 15371.40 thousand tonnes with the break up of 14740.55 thousand tonnes for cereals and 630.85 thousand tonnes for pulses.

The forecast of the production of the food grains production in Bihar at the expected range level in 2005-06 will be 13414.68 thousand tonnes which will further grow to 14502.84 thousand tonnes in 2010-11. There will be a phenomenal growth in the state in the production of cereals from 12902.97 thousand tonnes in 2005-06 to 14050.57 thousand tonnes in 2010-11. The production of pulses in 2005-06 is 511.71 thousand tonnes which further decreased to 452.27 thousand tonnes in 2010-11.

3.3.2 ESTIMATES OF POPULATION DISTRIBUTION BY AGE GROUPS

The estimated population distribution for the state of Bihar by different age groups required for the projection of food grains requirement for the year 2006 and 2011 is shown in Fig. 3.5 and 3.6.

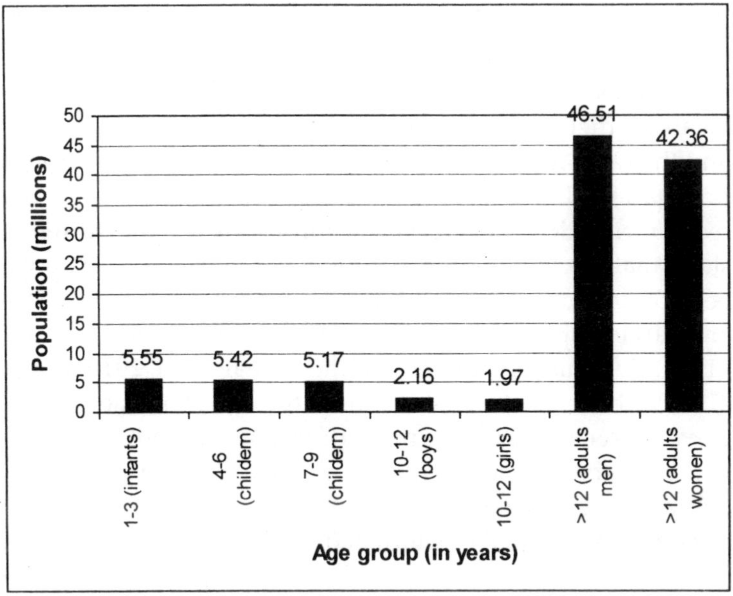

Fig. 3.5: Population distribution by age groups in 2006

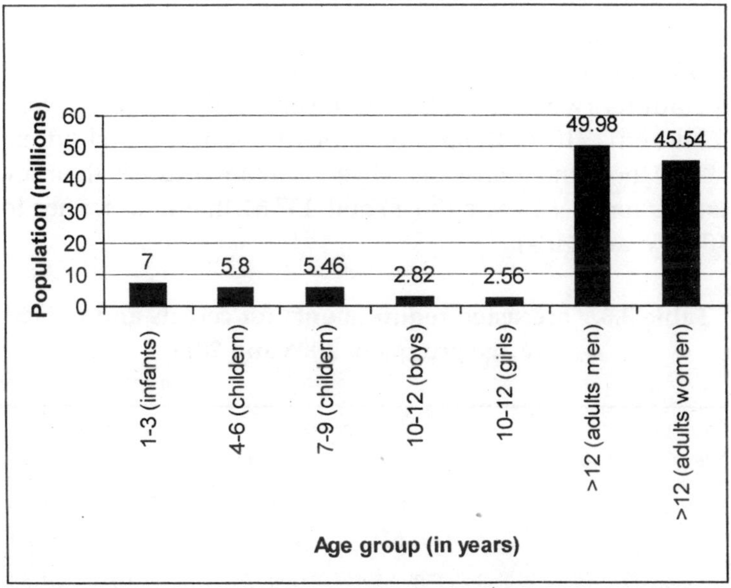

Fig. 3.6: Population distribution by age groups in 2011

3.3.3 PROJECTIONS OF FOOD GRAINS REQUIREMENT

The projections for food grain requirement by different age groups separately for cereals and pulses, on the basis of balanced diet has been estimated for the year 2006 and 2011 and the same is given in Table 3.6. On the basis of constructed population distribution by age groups and balanced diet recommendation for cereals and pulses, the estimated results show that the food grains requirement for the Bihar state will be 21554.48 and 23405.13 thousand tonnes for the year 2006 and 2011 respectively. The break up will be 19543.66 and 21214.22 thousand tonnes for the cereals and 2010.81 and 2190.90 thousand tonnes of pulses for the two time periods. The requirement for food grains in 2006 by different age groups will be highest in adults (men) i.e. 10642.77 thousand tonnes followed by 8249.74 thousand tonnes for adults (women), 790.86 thousand tonnes for 7-9 years (children), 663.71 thousand tonnes for 4-6 years (children) 467.95 thousand tonnes for 1-3 years (infants), 403.48 thousand tonnes for 10-12 years (boys) and 335.95 thousand tonnes for 10-12 years (girls). By the year 2011, the food grains requirement will be highest in adults (men) i.e. 11439.15 thousand tonnes followed by 8867.05 thousand tonnes for adults (women), 835.21 thousand tonnes for 7-9 years (children), 710.25 thousand tonnes for 4-6 years (children), 590.19 thousand tonnes for 1-3 years (infants), 525.60 thousand tonnes for 10-12 years (boys) and 437.64 thousand tonnes for 10-12 years (girls).

Table 3.6. Forecasted requirement* for cereals and pulses by age groups in 2006 and 2011

(in thousand tonnes)

Food groups	*Cereals*		*Pulses*	
Year /Age groups	*2006*	*2011*	*2006*	*2011*
1-3 years	389.96 (354.51)	491.83 (447.12)	77.99 (70.90)	98.36 (89.42)
4-6 years	587.55 (534.14)	628.75 (571.60)	76.16 (69.24)	81.50 (74.09)

7-9 years		707.83 (643.48)	747.53 (679.57)	83.03 (75.48)	87.68 (79.71)
10-12 years	Boys	364.44 (331.31)	474.74 (431.58)	39.04 (35.49)	50.86 (46.24)
	Girls	300.38 (273.07)	391.30 (355.73)	35.57 (32.34)	46.34 (42.13)
Adults	Men	9709.20 (8826.54)	10435.72 (9487.01)	933.57 (848.70)	1003.43 (912.21)
	Women	7484.30 (6803.91)	8044.33 (7313.02)	765.44 (695.85)	822.72 (747.93)
Total		19543.66 (17766.96)	21214.21 (19285.64)	2010.81 (1828.00)	2190.90 (1991.73)

*Forecasted requirement is at retail level.
Figure in parenthesis indicates the forecasted requirement at physiological level.

3.3.4 CONCLUSION

The estimates of food grains production and requirement indicated that overall cereals and pulses requirement would continue to be in deficit condition in both the periods. The total food grain deficit in 2005-06 will be 8139.79 thousand tonnes which increased to 8902.27 thousand tonnes in 2010–11. The net deficit of cereals and pulses in the state would be 6640.69 and 1499.10 thousand tonnes in 2005-06 and 7163.64 and 1738.63 thousand tonnes in 2010-11. The per capita per day availability of food grains, excluding 0 years population age group, in the state in year 2005-06 will be 336.74 grams which decreased to 333.44 grams in 2010-11.This clearly indicates that the population in the feeding age groups is increasing faster than the food grains production in the state. The estimated per capita per day availability of cereals would be 323.90 and 323.05 grams for the year 2005-06 and 2010-11 while the per capita per day availability of pulses is 12.83 and 10.40 grams for the same time periods. The estimated ranges i.e. pessimistic range and optimistic range in which the per capita per day availability for cereals may vary is 310.88 to 336.92 grams and 307.19 to 338.91 grams for the year 2005-06 and 2010-11. The estimated limits for the pulses is 9.95 to 15.74 grams and 6.29 to 14.50 grams for the same periods.

3.4
GUJARAT

The state of Gujarat has total geographical area of about 19,598 thousand hectares with population of the state, as per census 2001, is 50,671,017 out of which about 37.4% of population resides in urban area. The sex ratio (i.e. females per thousand males) and population density (average number of persons per sq km) is 920 and 258 respectively. The total literacy rate in state is 69.1% which comprises 79.7% for male as against 57.8% for females. The state of Gujarat is situated on the west coast of the country. The state is bounded by Rajasthan in the north Madhya Pradesh in the east, Maharashtra in the south-east, Arabian Sea in the west and Pakistan in the north-west.

The state is a leading producer of the crops like groundnut, cotton and onion. The other major crops include rice, wheat, maize, tobacco, fruits, vegetables and spices. The major crops of horticulture in Gujarat are banana, mango, chikoo and papaya. The major vegetable crops grown in Gujarat are onion, potato, brinjal and tomato. In addition to this, Gujarat also produces chillies, cumin, fennel and garlic. In India, Gujarat ranks third in the production of banana, sixth in production of mango, second in papaya and chikoo production.

3.4.1 PROJECTIONS OF FOOD GRAINS PRODUCTION

The projections of food grains separately for the cereals and pulses for the state of Gujarat at lower (pessimistic), expected (normal) and upper (optimistic) level for the year 2005-06 and 2010-11 is presented in the Table 3.7.

Table 3.7: Forecasted production of cereals and pulses for the year 2005-06 and 2010-11

(in thousand tonnes)

Food groups		*Cereals*		*Pulses*	
Year /Age groups		*2005-06*	*2010-11*	*2005-06*	*2010-11*
Forecasted gross production		5603.16	6213.66	776.88	877.63
95% forecasted gross production prediction interval		5603.16 ± 537.98	6213.66 ± 715.52	776.88 ±69.43	877.63 ±42.75
Forecasted net production	Lower range level	4432.03	4810.87	619.01	730.52
	Expected range level	4902.76	5436.95	679.77	767.92
	Upper range level	5373.49	6063.03	740.52	805.33

The scrutiny of Table 3.7 reveals that the production of food grains in 2005-06 at lower range level will be 5051.04 thousand tonnes with break up of 4432.03 thousand tonnes for cereals and 619.01 thousand tonnes for the pulses. By the year 2010-11, the production will be 5541.39 thousand tonnes with the break up of 4810.87 thousand tonnes for cereals and 730.52 thousand tonnes for pulses.

At upper range level, the production of food grains in 2005-06 will be 6114.01 thousand tonnes with break up of 5373.49 thousand tonnes for cereals and 740.52 thousand tonnes for pulses. By the year 2010-11, the production will be 6868.36 thousand tonnes with the break up of 6063.03 thousand tonnes for cereals and 805.33 thousand tonnes for pulses.

The forecast of food grains production in Gujarat at the expected range level in 2005-06 will be 5582.53 thousand tonnes which will further grow to 6204.87 thousand tonnes in 2010-11. There will be a growth in the production of cereals from 4902.76 thousand tonnes in 2005-06 to 5436.95 thousand tonnes in 2010-11. The production of pulses in 2005-06 is 679.77 thousand tonnes which increases to 767.92 thousand tonnes in 2010-11.

3.4.2 ESTIMATES OF POPULATION DISTRIBUTION BY AGE GROUPS

The estimated population distribution for the state of Gujarat by different age groups required for the projection of food grains requirement for the year 2006 and 2011is shown in Fig. 3.7 and 3.8.

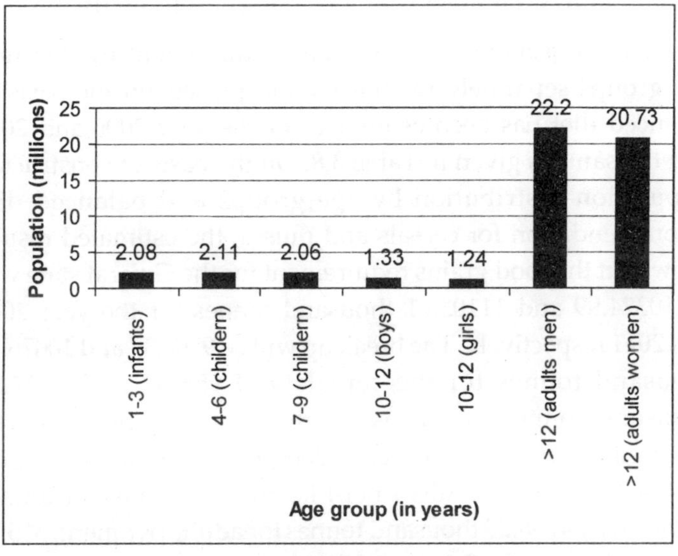

Fig. 3.7: Population distribution by age groups in 2006

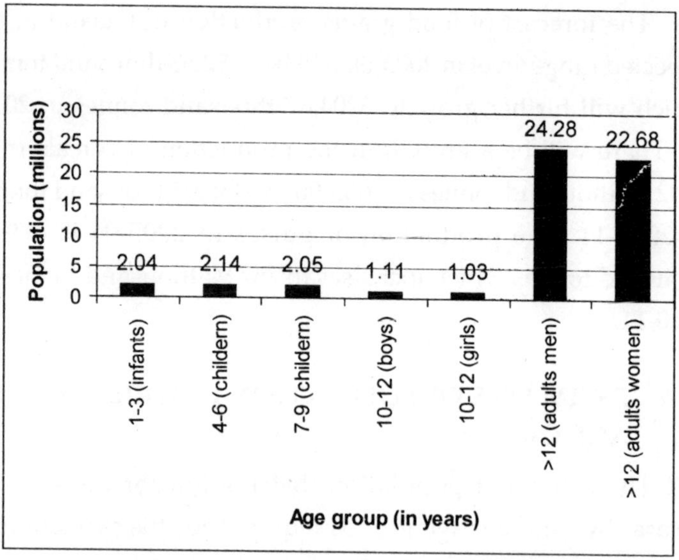

Fig. 3.8: Population distribution by age groups in 2011

3.4.3 PROJECTIONS OF FOOD GRAINS REQUIREMENT

The projections for food grain requirement by different age groups separately for cereals and pulses, on the basis of balanced diet has been estimated for the year 2006 and 2011 and the same is given in Table 3.8. On the basis of constructed population distribution by age groups and balanced diet recommendation for cereals and pulses, the estimated results show that the food grains requirement for the Gujarat state will be 10324.99 and 11103.61 thousand tonnes for the year 2006 and 2011 respectively. The break up will be 9366.37 and 10076.11 thousand tonnes for the cereals and 958.62 and 1027.50 thousand tonnes of pulses for the two time periods. The requirement for food grains in 2006 by different age groups will be highest in adults (men) i.e 5078.83 thousand tonnes followed by 4036.29 thousand tonnes for adults (women), 315.12 thousand tonnes for 7-9 years (children), 258.38 thousand tonnes for 4-6 years (children), 248.38 thousand tonnes for 10-12 years (boys), 212.61 thousand tonnes for 10-12 years (girls) and 175.38 thousand tonnes for 1-3 years (infants). By the year 2011, the food grains requirement will be highest in adults (men) i.e. 5556.88 thousand tonnes followed by 4416.17 thousand tonnes for adults (women), 313.59 thousand tonnes for 7-9 years (children), 262.05 thousand tonnes for 4-6 years (children), 206.58 thousand tonnes for 10-12 years (boys), 176.35 thousand tonnes for 10-12 years (girls) and 171.99 thousand tonnes for 1-3 years (infants).

Table 3.8. Forecasted requirement* for cereals and pulses by age groups in 2006 and 2011

(in thousand tonnes)

Food groups		*Cereals*		*Pulses*	
Year/Age groups		*2006*	*2011*	*2006*	*2011*
1-3 years		146.15 (132.86)	143.33 (130.30)	29.23 (26.57)	28.66 (26.05)
4-6 years		228.73 (207.94)	231.98 (210.89)	29.65 (26.95)	30.07 (27.34)
7-9 years		282.04 (256.40)	280.67 (255.15)	33.08 (30.07)	32.92 (29.93)
10-12 years	Boys	224.28 (203.89)	186.59 (169.63)	24.10 (21.91)	19.99 (18.17)
	Girls	190.10 (172.82)	157.68 (143.34)	22.51 (20.46)	18.67 (16.97)
Adults	Men	4633.32 (4212.11)	5069.44 (4608.58)	445.51 (405.01)	487.44 (443.13)
	Women	3661.75 (3328.86)	4006.42 (3642.20)	374.54 (340.49)	409.75 (372.50)
Total		9366.37 (8514.88)	10076.11 (9160.10)	958.62 (871.47)	1027.50 (934.09)

*Forecasted requirement is at retail level.
Figure in parenthesis indicates the forecasted requirement at physiological level.

3.4.4 CONCLUSION

The estimates of food grains production and requirement indicated that overall cereals and pulses requirement would continue to be in deficit condition in both the periods. The net deficit of cereals in the state would be 4463.61 and 4639.16 thousand tonnes in 2005-06 and 2010-11. The net deficit of pulses in the state would be 278.85 and 259.58 thousand tonnes in the same periods. The per capita per day availability of food grains, excluding 0 years population age group, in the state in year 2005-06 will be 295.55 grams which decreased to 307.24 grams in 2010-11. The estimated per capita per day availability (excluding 0 years population age group) of cereals would be 259.56 and 269.22 grams for the year 2005-06 and 2010-11 while the per capita per day availability of pulses is 35.99 and 38.02 for the same time periods. The estimated ranges i.e. pessimistic range and optimistic range in which the per capita per day availability for cereals may vary is 234.68 to 284.48 grams and 238.21 to 300.22 grams for the year 2005-06 and 2010-11. The estimated limits for the pulses is 32.77 to 39.20 grams and 36.17 to 39.88 grams for the same periods.

3.5
HARYANA

The state of Haryana has total geographical area of about 4,422 thousand hectares. The population of the state, as per census 2001, is 21,144,564 out of which about 28.9% of population resides in urban area. The sex ratio (i.e. females per thousand males) and population density (average number of persons per sq km) is 861 and 478 respectively. The total literacy rate in state is 67.9% which comprises 78.5% for male as against 55.7% for females.The state is located in the northwest part of the country. The state is bounded by Uttar Pradesh in east, Punjab in west, Himachal Pradesh in north and Rajasthan in south.The climate of state is arid to semi arid.

Apart from meeting its own requirement for food grains, the state of Haryana also contributes large amount of food grains to the Central Pool annually and therefore helps in improving the food security status of the country. The Basmati rice produced in Haryana has significance in export. There are two agro climatic zones in the state. The north western part is suitable for rice, wheat, vegetable and temperate fruits and the south western part is suitable for high quality agricultural produce, tropical fruits, exotic vegetables, herbal and medicinal plants. Nearly 86% of the geographical area is cultivable, out of which, about 96% is under plough.

3.5.1 PROJECTIONS OF FOOD GRAINS PRODUCTION

The projections of food grains separately for the cereals and pulses for the state of Haryana at lower (pessimistic), expected (normal) and upper (optimistic) level for the year 2005-06 and 2010-11 is presented in the Table 3.9.

Table 3.9: Forecasted production of cereals and pulses for the year 2005-06 and 2010-11.

(in thousand tonnes)

Food groups		*Cereals*		*Pulses*	
Year /Production		*2005-06*	*2010-11*	*2005-06*	*2010-11*
Forecasted gross production		14168.86	16032.56	395.78	395.78
95% forecasted gross production prediction interval		14168.86 ± 1704.37	16032.56 ± 1899.02	395.78 ± 142.60	395.78 ± 136.80
Forecasted net production	Lower range level	10906.42	12366.84	221.53	226.60
	Expected range level	12397.75	14028.49	346.30	346.30
	Upper range level	13889.07	15690.13	471.08	446.02

The scrutiny of Table 3.9 reveals that the production of food grains in 2005-06 at lower range level will be 11127.95 thousand tonnes with break up of 10906.42 thousand tonnes for cereals and 221.53 thousand tonnes for the pulses. By the year 2010-11, the production will be 12593.44 thousand tonnes with the break up of 12366.84 thousand tonnes for cereals and 226.60 thousand tonnes for pulses.

At upper range level, the production of food grains in 2005-06 will be 14360.15 thousand tonnes with break up of 13889.07 thousand tonnes for cereals and 471.08 thousand tonnes for pulses. By the year 2010-11, the production will be 16136.15 thousand tonnes with the break up of 15690.13 thousand tonnes for cereals and 446.02 thousand tonnes for pulses.

The food grains production in Haryana at the expected range level in 2005-06 will be 12744.05 thousand tonnes which will further grow to 14374.79 thousand tonnes in 2010-11. There will be a phenomenal growth in the state in the production of cereals from 12397.75 thousand tonnes in 2005-06 to 14028.49 thousand tonnes in 2010-11. The production of pulses in 2005-06 is 346.30 thousand tonnes and shows same stagnancy level in 2010-11.

3.5.2 ESTIMATES OF POPULATION DISTRIBUTION BY AGE GROUPS

The estimated population distribution for the state of Haryana by different age groups required for the projection of food grains requirement for the year 2006 and 2011 is shown in Fig. 3.9 and 3.10.

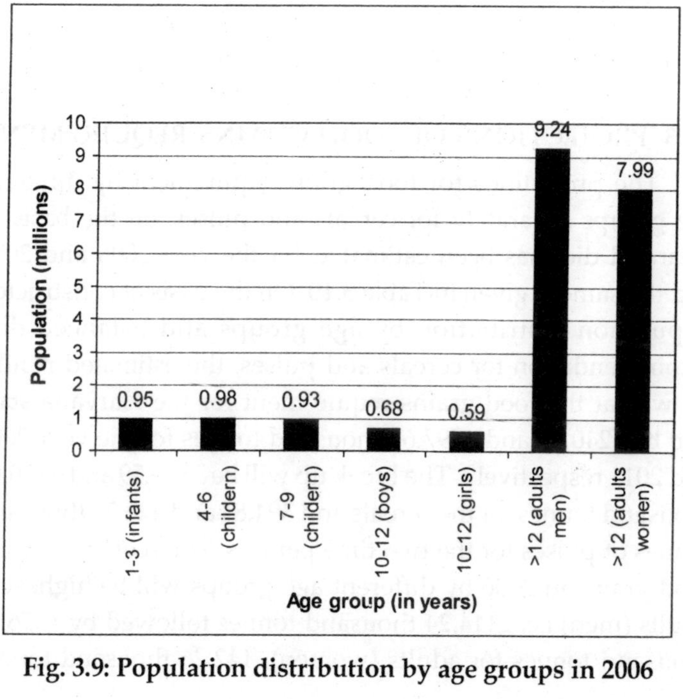

Fig. 3.9: Population distribution by age groups in 2006

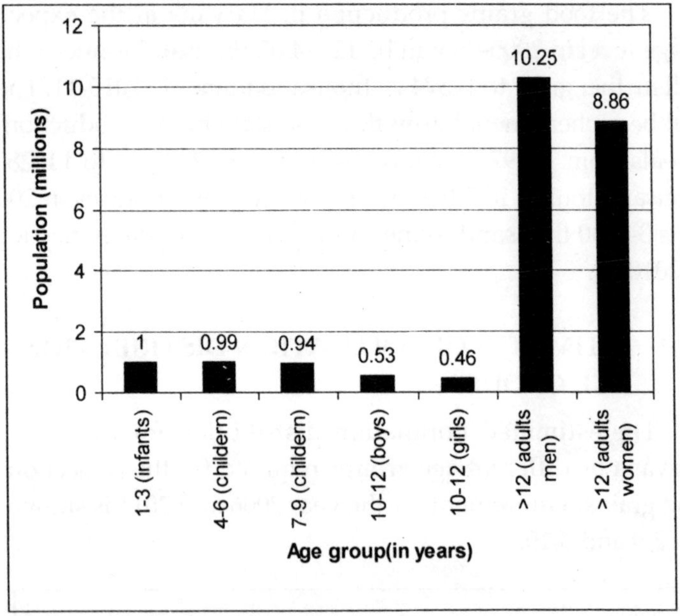

Fig. 3.10: Population distribution by age groups in 2011

3.5.3 PROJECTIONS OF FOOD GRAINS REQUIREMENT

The projections for food grain requirement by different age groups separately for cereals and pulses, on the basis of balanced diet has been estimated for the year 2006 and 2011 and the same is given in Table 3.10. On the basis of constructed population distribution by age groups and balanced diet recommendation for cereals and pulses, the estimated results show that the food grains requirement for the Haryana state will be 4240.43 and 4597.64 thousand tonnes for the year 2006 and 2011 respectively. The break up will be 3845.59 and 4170.87 thousand tonnes for the cereals and 394.84 and 426.77 thousand tonnes of pulses for the two time periods. The requirement for food grains in 2006 by different age groups will be highest in adults (men) i.e. 2114.24 thousand tonnes followed by 1556.19 thousand tonnes for adults (women), 142.26 thousand tonnes for 7-9 years (children), 127.12 thousand tonnes for 10-12 years (boys), 120.01 thousand tonnes for 4-6 years (children), 100.51 thousand tonnes for 10-12 years (girls) and 80.1 thousand tonnes for 1-3 years (infants). By the year 2011, the food grains requirement will be highest in adults (men) i.e.2344.92 thousand tonnes followed by 1725.99 thousand tonnes for adults (women), 143.80 thousand tonnes for 7-9 years (children), 121.23 thousand tonnes for 4-6 years (children), 99.10 thousand tonnes for 10-12 years (boys), 78.35 thousand tonnes for 10-12 years (girls) and 84.31 thousand tonnes for 1-3 years (infants).

Table 3.10. Forecasted requirement* for cereals and pulses by age groups in 2006 and 2011

(in thousand tonnes)

Food groups		*Cereals*		*Pulses*	
Year /Age groups		*2006*	*2011*	*2006*	*2011*
1-3 years		66.75 (60.68)	70.26 (63.87)	13.35 (12.13)	14.05 (12.77)
4-6 years		106.24 (96.58)	107.32 (97.56)	13.77 (12.52)	13.91 (12.64)
7-9 years		127.33 (115.75)	128.70 (117.04)	14.93 (13.57)	15.10 (13.72)
10-12 years	Boys	114.82 (104.38)	89.51 (81.37)	12.30 (11.18)	9.59 (8.72)
	Girls	89.87 (81.70)	70.06 (63.69)	10.64 (9.67)	8.29 (7.53)
Adults	Men	1928.78 (1753.43)	2139.23 (1944.75)	185.46 (168.60)	205.69 (186.99)
	Women	1411.80 (1283.45)	1565.85 (1423.50)	144.39 (131.26)	160.14 (145.58)
Total		3845.59 (3495.99)	4170.87 (3791.70)	394.84 (358.94)	426.77 (387.97)

*Forecasted requirement is at retail level.

Figure in parenthesis indicates the forecasted requirement at physiological level.

3.5.4 CONCLUSION

It is observed that the state of Haryana has a wide role to provide the food security to the nation. The estimates of food grains production and requirement indicated that overall there will be large surplus in case of cereals while the pulses requirement will continue to be in deficit condition due to stagnant growth rate of production. The total food grain surplus in 2005-06 will be 8503.62 thousand tonnes which increased to 9777.15 thousand tonnes in 2010 – 11. The net surplus of cereals available in the state will be 8552.16 and 9857.62 thousand tonnes, which is about 68.98 and 70.27% of net forecasted production at expected range level for the year 2005-06 and 2010-11 respectively. The per capita per day availability of food grains, excluding 0 years population age group, in the state in year 2005-06 will be 1634.61 grams which increased to 1710.08 grams in 2010-11. The estimated per capita per day availability (excluding 0 years population age group) of cereals would be 1590.19 and 1668.88 grams for the year 2005-06 and 2010-11 while the per capita per day availability of pulses is 44.42 and 41.20 for the same time periods. The estimated ranges i.e. pessimistic range and optimistic range in which the per capita per day availability for cereals may vary is 1398.90 to 1781.47 grams and 1471.20 to 1866.55 grams for the year 2005-06 and 2010-11. The estimated limits for the pulses is 28.41 to 60.42 grams and 29.96 to 53.06 grams for the same periods.

3.6
HIMACHAL PRADESH

The state of Himachal Pradesh spreads about 5,567 thousand hectare of area. The population of the state, as per census 2001, is 6,077,900 out of which about 9.8% of population resides in urban area. The sex ratio (i.e. females per thousand males) and population density (average number of persons per sq km) 968 is and 109 respectively. The total literacy rate in state is 76.5% which comprises 85.3% for male as against 67.4% for females. The state extends between 30°22' and 30°12' north latitude and 75°47' to 79°04' east longitude, spreading from Shivalik hills to great Himalayas ranges in the north. The state is bordered by Jammu and Kashmir in north, Punjab in west and south west, Haryana in south, Uttar Pradesh in south east and by Tibet in east.

The agriculture is major sector (compared to the industry sector), which provides the employment and income to the peoples of hilly region, as large-scale industrialization is neither physically possible nor ecologically desirable in hills. The low valley areas are plain fertile and suitable for intensive cultivation of cereal and vegetable crops while high hills are suitable for apples and dry fruits.The state is deficit in food grains and suffers from certain limitation in the production of these crops. The main reason is that net cultivated area, as the proportion of total geographical area (10-11%) is very small in Himachal Pradesh, which also has undulated topography and steep slope and also cannot be extended to the appreciable extent. Nearly 80 % area of the total cultivated area in the state is rain fed. Rice, wheat and maize are important cereal crops while urd, bean, moong, rajmash in kharif season and gram, lentil in Rabi are important pulse crop of the state. Maize is the potential crop of mid and low hills, occupying largest area and production during Kharif season. The average holding size comes to 1.2 hectares and about 84.5% of the total holdings are of small and marginal farmers. The agro climatic conditions of various zones of Himachal Pradesh are suited for the production of the production of various types of sub-tropical, temperate fruits and off-season vegetables.

3.6.1 PROJECTIONS OF FOOD GRAINS PRODUCTION

The projections of food grains separately for the cereals and pulses for the state of Himachal Pradesh at lower (pessimistic), expected (normal) and upper (optimistic) level for the year 2005-06 and 2010-11 is presented in the Table 3.11.

Table 3.11: Forecasted production of cereals and pulses for the year 2005-06 and 2010-11.

(in thousand tonnes)

Food groups		*Cereals*		*Pulses*	
Year /Production		*2005-06*	*2010-11*	*2005-06*	*2010-11*
Forecasted gross production		1534.31	1623.16	14.84	16.34
95% forecasted gross production prediction interval		1534.31 ± 199.72	1623.16 ± 193.68	14.84 ± 1.25	16.34 ± 1.67
Forecasted net production	Lower range level	1167.76	1250.79	11.89	12.83
	Expected range level	1342.52	1420.26	12.98	14.29
	Upper range level	1517.27	1589.73	14.07	15.75

The scrutiny of Table 3.11 reveals that the production of food grains in 2005-06 at lower range level will be 1179.65 thousand tonnes with break up of 1167.76 thousand tonnes for cereals and 11.89 thousand tonnes for the pulses. By the year 2010-11, the production will be 1263.62 thousand tonnes with the break up of 1250.79 thousand tonnes for cereals and 12.83 thousand tonnes for pulses.

At upper range level, the production of food grains in 2005-06 will be 1531.34 thousand tonnes with break up of 1517.27 thousand tonnes for cereals and 14.07 thousand tonnes for pulses. By the year 2010-11, the production will be 1605.48 thousand tonnes with the break up of 1589.73 thousand tonnes for cereals and 15.75 thousand tonnes for pulses.

The forecasting of food grains production in Himachal Pradesh at the expected range level in 2005-06 will be 1355.50 thousand tonnes which will further grow to 1434.55 thousand tonnes in 2010-11. The production of cereals increased from 1342.52 thousand tonnes in 2005-06 to 1420.26 thousand tonnes in 2010-11. The production of pulses increased from 12.98 thousand tonnes to 14.29 thousand tonnes in the same period.

3.6.2 ESTIMATES OF POPULATION DISTRIBUTION BY AGE GROUPS

The estimated population distribution for the state of Himachal Pradesh by different age groups required for the projection of food grains requirements for the year 2006 and 2011 is shown in Fig. 3.11 and 3.12.

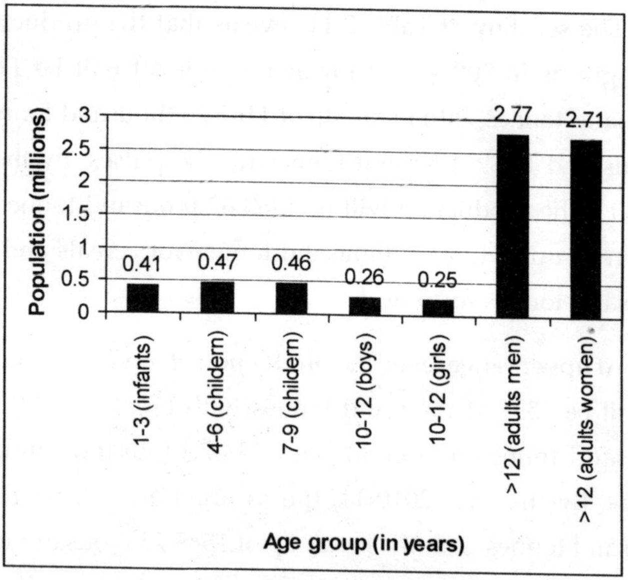

Fig. 3.11: Population distribution by age groups in 2006

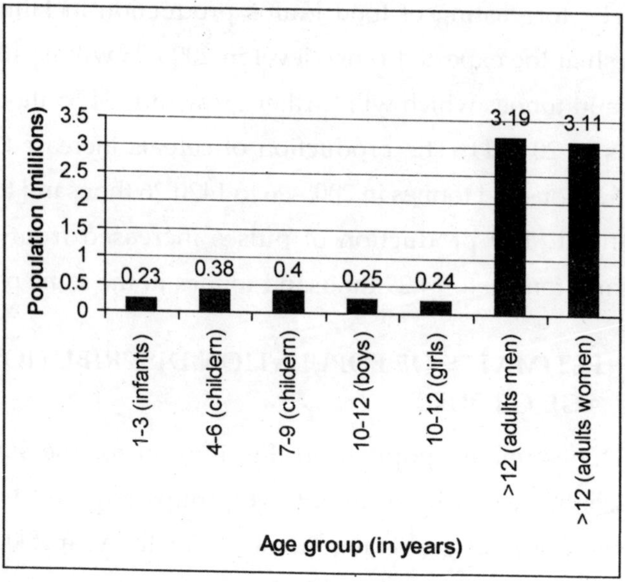

Fig. 3.12: Population distribution by age groups in 2011

3.6.3 PROJECTIONS OF FOOD GRAINS REQUIREMENT

The projections for food grain requirement by different age groups separately for cereals and pulses, on the basis of balanced diet has been estimated for the year 2006 and 2011 and the same is given in Table 3.12. On the basis of constructed population distribution by age groups and balanced diet recommendation for cereals and pulses, the estimated results show that the food grains requirement for the Himachal Pradesh state will be 1417.19 and 1552.07 thousand tonnes for the year 2006 and 2011 respectively. The break up will be 1283.47 and 1407.82 thousand tonnes for the cereals and 133.72 and 144.25 thousand tonnes of pulses for the two time periods. The requirement for food grains in 2006 by different age groups will be highest in adults (men) i.e. 634.67 thousand tonnes followed by 527.07 thousand tonnes for adults (women), 70.37 thousand tonnes for 7-9 years children, 57.56 thousand tonnes for 4-6 years (children), 49.13 thousand tonnes for 10-12 years (boys), 43.82 thousand tonnes for 10-12 years (girls) and 34.57 thousand tonnes for 1-3 years (infants). By the year 2011, the food grains requirement will be highest in adults (men) i.e. 729.64 thousand tonnes followed by 605.94 thousand tonnes for adults (women), 61.19 thousand tonnes for 7-9 years (children), 47.24 thousand tonnes for 10-12 years (boys), 46.53 thousand tonnes for 4-6 years (children), 42.14 thousand tonnes for 10-12 years (girls) and 19.39 thousand tonnes for 1-3 years (infants).

Table 3.12. Forecasted requirement* for cereals and pulses by age groups in 2006 and 2011

(in thousand tonnes)

Crop groups	*Cereals*		*Pulses*	
Year/Age groups	*2005-06*	*2010-11*	*2005-06*	*2010-11*
1-3 years	28.81 (26.19)	16.16 (14.69)	5.76 (5.24)	3.23 (2.94)

4-6 years		50.95 (46.32)	41.19 (37.44)	6.61 (6.00)	5.34 (4.85)
7-9 years		62.98 (57.25)	54.76 (49.78)	7.39 (6.72)	6.43 (5.84)
10-12 years	Boys	44.38 (40.34)	42.67 (38.79)	4.75 (4.32)	4.57 (4.15)
	Girls	39.18 (35.62)	37.68 (34.25)	4.64 (4.22)	4.46 (4.05)
Adults	Men	579.00 (526.36)	665.64 (605.13)	55.67 (50.61)	64.00 (58.18)
	Women	478.17 (434.70)	549.72 (499.74)	48.90 (44.45)	56.22 (51.11)
Total		1283.47 (1166.79)	1407.82 (1279.84)	133.72 (121.56)	144.25 (131.14)

*Forecasted requirement is at retail level.
Figure in parenthesis indicates the forecasted requirement at physiological level.

6.3.4 CONCLUSION

The estimates of food grains production and requirement indicated that there will be marginal surplus in case of cereals while pulses will remain in deficit condition. The total food grain deficit in 2005-06 will be 61.69 thousand tonnes, which increased to 117.52 thousand tonnes in 2010–11. The net surplus of cereals available in the state will be 59.05 and 12.44 thousand tonnes, which are about 4.4 and 0.87% of net forecasted production at expected range level for the year 2005-06 and 2010-11 respectively. If it is assumed that the consumption in the state is as per the balanced diet norms and distribution is proper with no constraints of purchasing power then it is the available markeTable surplus of cereals. However in case of pulses, the situation is different and the deficit of pulses is 120.74 and 129.96 thousand tonnes for the year 2005-

06 and 2010-11. In this situation the state needs to expand the production either by increasing production or area or both. The per capita per day availability of food grains, excluding 0 years population age group, in the state in year 2005-06 will be 507.33 grams which decreased to 503.88 grams in 2010-11. The estimated per capita per day availability of cereals would be 502.47 and 498.86 grams for the year 2005-06 and 2010-11 while the per capita per day availability of pulses is 4.86 and 5.02 for the same time periods. The estimated ranges i.e. pessimistic range and optimistic range in which the per capita per day availability for cereals may vary is 437.07 to 567.88 grams and 439.34 to 558.39 grams for the year 2005-06 and 2010-11. The estimated limits for the pulses is 4.45 to 5.27 grams and 4.51 to 5.53 grams for the same periods.

3.7
JAMMU AND KASHMIR

The population of the state of Jammu and Kashmir as per census 2001, is 10,143,700, out of which about 24.8% of population resides in urban area. The sex ratio (i.e. females per thousand males) and population density (average number of persons per sq km) is 892 and 100 respectively. The total literacy rate in state is 55.5% which comprises 66.6% for male as against 43.0% for females. The state of Jammu and Kashmir is situated in the extreme north. Its boundaries is covered by Tibet in east, Punjab and Himachal Pradesh in south and Pakistan in west.

The state of Jammu and Kashmir is primarily an agricultural state and most of the population lives in villages. Rice, maize, and wheat are the major crops and fruits like apples, pears, apricots, almonds, walnuts, peaches and cherries grow in abundance. The valley is also rich in forests which play a key role in maintaining the ecological balance. Mulberry trees grow in abundance and are the mainstay of silk industry in the Valley. The state is predominantly a mono-cropped and rainfed economy with about 40% of the area in Jammu division and 60% in Kashmir division having assured means of irrigation. Agriculture is one of the key factors and the mainstay of the state's economy. The productivity level of paddy at about 40 quintals per hectare in Kashmir valley is the highest in the country.

3.7.1 PROJECTIONS OF FOOD GRAINS PRODUCTION

The projections of food grains separately for the cereals and pulses for the state of Jammu and Kashmir at lower (pessimistic), expected (normal) and upper (optimistic) level for the year 2005-06 and 2010-11 is presented in the Table 3.13.

Table 3.13: Forecasted production of cereals and pulses for the year 2005-06 and 2010-11

(in thousand tonnes)

Crop groups		*Cereals*		*Pulses*	
Year /Production		*2005-06*	*2010-11*	*2005-06*	*2010-11*
Forecasted gross production		1571.71	1664.93	9.90	5.66
95% forecasted gross production prediction interval		1571.71 ± 53.61	1664.95 ± 71.32	9.90 ± 1.62	5.66 ± 2.16
Forecasted net production	Lower range level	1328.34	1394.42	7.24	3.06
	Expected range level	1375.24	1456.83	8.66	4.95
	Upper range level	1422.15	1519.22	10.08	7.28

The scrutiny of Table 3.13 reveals that the production of food grains in 2005-06 at lower range level will be 1335.58 thousand tonnes with break up of 1328.34 thousand tonnes for cereals and 7.24 thousand tonnes for the pulses. By the year 2010-11, the production will be 1397.48 thousand tonnes with the break up of 1394.42 thousand tonnes for cereals and 3.06 thousand tonnes for pulses.

At upper range level, the production of food grains in 2005-06 will be 1432.23 thousand tonnes with break up of 1422.15 thousand tonnes for cereals and 10.08 thousand tonnes for pulses. By the year 2010-11, the production will be 1526.50 thousand tonnes with the break up of 1519.22 thousand tonnes for cereals and 7.28 thousand tonnes for pulses.

The food grains production in Jammu and Kashmir at the expected range level in 2005-06 will be 1383.9 thousand tonnes which will further grow to 1461.78 thousand tonnes in 2010-11. There will be a growth in the production of cereals from 1375.24 thousand tonnes in 2005-06 to 1456.83 thousand tonnes in 2010-11. The production of pulses in 2005-06 is 8.66 thousand tonnes which declined to 4.95 thousand tonnes in 2010-11.

3.7.2 ESTIMATES OF POPULATION DISTRIBUTION BY AGE GROUPS

The estimated population distribution for the state of Jammu and Kashmir by different age groups required for the projection of food grains requirement for the year 2006 and 2011 is shown in Fig. 3.13 and 3.14.

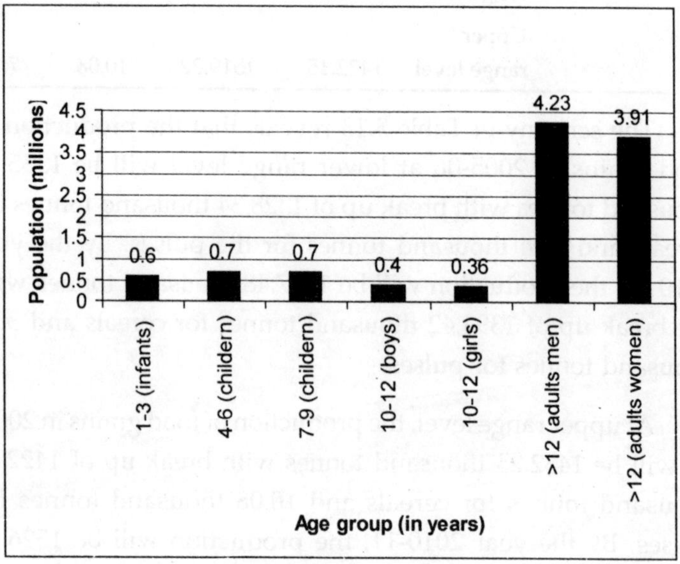

Fig. 3.13: Population distribution by age groups in 2006

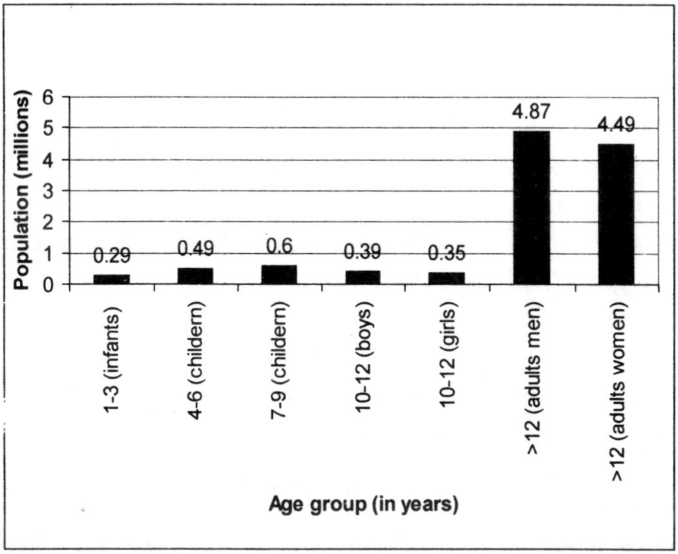

Fig. 3.14: Population distribution by age groups in 2011

3.7.3 PROJECTIONS OF FOOD GRAINS REQUIREMENT

The projections for food grain requirement by different age groups separately for cereals and pulses, on the basis of balanced diet has been estimated for the year 2006 and 2011 and the same is given in Table 3.14. On the basis of constructed population distribution by age groups and balanced diet recommendation for cereals and pulses, the estimated results show that the food grains requirement for the Jammu and Kashmir state will be 2108.87 and 2297.42 thousand tonnes for the year 2006 and 2011 respectively.The break up will be 1910.13 and 2084.58 thousand tonnes for the cereals and 198.74 and 212.84 thousand tonnes of pulses for the two time periods. The requirement for food grains in 2006 by different age groups will be highest in adults (men) i.e. 968.73 thousand tonnes followed by 760.72 thousand tonnes for adults (women), 107.07 thousand tonnes for 7-9 years (children), 85.72 thousand tonnes for 4-6 years (children), 73.78 thousand tonnes for 10-12 years (boys), 62.25 thousand tonnes for 10-12 years (girls) and 50.60 thousand tonnes for 1-3 years (infants). By the year 2011, the food grains requirement will be highest in adults (men) i.e.1113.92 thousand tonnes followed by 874.83 thousand tonnes for adults (women), 91.78 thousand tonnes for 7-9 years (children), 71.84 thousand tonnes for 10-12 years (boys), 60.61 thousand tonnes for 10-12 years (girls), 60.0 thousand tonnes for 4-6 years (children) and 24.44 thousand tonnes for 1-3 years (infants).

Table 3.14. Forecasted requirement* for cereals and pulses by age groups in 2006 and 2011

(in thousand tonnes)

Food groups		*Cereals*		*Pulses*	
Year/Age groups		*2005-06*	*2010-11*	*2005-06*	*2010-11*
1-3 years		42.16	20.37	8.44	4.07
		(38.33)	(18.52)	(7.67)	(3.70)
4-6 years		75.88	53.12	9.84	6.88
		(68.98)	(48.29)	(8.94)	(6.25)
7-9 years		95.83	82.14	11.24	9.64
		(87.12)	(74.67)	(10.22)	(8.76)
10-12 years	Boys	66.64	64.89	7.14	6.95
		(60.58)	(58.99)	(6.49)	(6.32)
	Girls	55.65	54.19	6.60	6.42
		(50.59)	(49.26)	(6.00)	(5.84)
Adults	Men	883.76	1016.21	84.97	97.71
		(803.42)	(923.83)	(77.24)	(88.83)
	Women	690.21	793.66	70.51	81.17
		(627.46)	(721.51)	(64.10)	(73.79)
Total		1910.13	2084.58	198.74	212.84
		(1736.48)	(1895.07)	(180.67)	(193.49)

*Forecasted requirement is at retail level.

Figure in parenthesis indicates the forecasted requirement at physiological level.

3.7.4 CONCLUSION

The estimates of food grains production and requirement indicated that overall cereals and pulses requirement would continue to be in deficit condition in both the periods. The total food grain deficit in 2005-06 will be 724.97 thousand tonnes which increased to 835.64 thousand tonnes in 2010-11. The net deficit of cereals in the state would be 534.89 and 627.75 thousand tonnes in 2005-06 and 2010-11 and 190.08 and 207.89 thousand tonnes for pulses in the same periods. The estimated per capita per day availability (excluding 0 years population age group) of cereals would be 345.67 and 347.67 grams for the year 2005-06 and 2010-11 while the per capita per day availability of pulses is 2.18 and 1.18 grams for the same time periods. The estimated ranges i.e. pessimistic range and optimistic range in which the per capita per day availability for cereals may vary is 333.88 to 357.46 grams and 332.78 to 362.56 grams for the year 2005-06 and 2010-11. The estimated limits for the pulses is 1.82 to 2.53 grams and 0.73 to 1.74 grams for the same periods.

3.8
KARNATAKA

The state of Karnataka has total geographical area of about 19,177 thousand hectares. The population of the state, as per census 2001, is 52,850,562 out of which about 34.0% of population resides in urban area. The sex ratio (i.e. females per thousand males) and population density (average number of persons per sq km) is 965 and 276 respectively. The total literacy rate in state is 66.6% which comprises 76.1% for male as against 56.9% for females. Karnataka is situated to the south of Goa and Maharashtra, to the west of Andhra Pradesh and Tamil Nadu and to the north of Kerala.

Agriculture and allied activities account for nearly 65% of the work force in the state. Important food crops are maize, paddy, jowar, ragi, bajra, wheat and pulses. The state ranks first in sun flower production and has the largest area planted under coffee.

3.8.1 PROJECTIONS OF FOOD GRAINS PRODUCTION

The projections of food grains separately for the cereals and pulses for the state of Karnataka at lower (pessimistic), expected (normal) and upper (optimistic) level for the year 2005-06 and 2010-11 is presented in the Table 3.15.

Table 3.15: Forecasted production of cereals and pulses for the year 2005-06 and 2010-11.

(in thousand tonnes)

Crop groups	*Cereals*		*Pulses*	
Year /Production	*2005-06*	*2010-11*	*2005-06*	*2010-11*
Forecasted gross production	10069.38	11114.48	822.23	915.83

95% forecasted gross production prediction interval		10069.38 ± 325.93	11114.48 ± 433.49	822.23 ± 40.69	915.85 ± 54.12
Forecasted net production	Lower range level	8525.52	9345.86	683.84	754.00
	Expected range level	8810.71	9725.17	719.45	801.36
	Upper range level	9095.89	10104.47	755.05	848.72

The scrutiny of Table 3.15 reveals that the production of food grains in 2005-06 at lower range level will be 9209.36 thousand tonnes with break up of 8525.52 thousand tonnes for cereals and 683.84 thousand tonnes for the pulses. By the year 2010-11, the production will be 10099.86 thousand tonnes with the break up of 9345.86 thousand tonnes for cereals and 754.00 thousand tonnes for pulses.

At upper range level, the production of food grains in 2005-06 will be 9850.94 thousand tonnes with break up of 9095.89 thousand tonnes for cereals and 755.05 thousand tonnes for pulses. By the year 2010-11, the production will be 10953.19 thousand tonnes with the break up of 10104.47 thousand tonnes for cereals and 848.72 thousand tonnes for pulses.

The food grains production in Karnataka at the expected range level in 2005-06 will be 9530.16 thousand tonnes which will further grow to 10526.53 thousand tonnes in 2010-11. There will be a growth in the production of cereals from 8810.71 thousand tonnes in 2005-06 to 9725.17 thousand tonnes in 2010-11. The production of pulses in 2005-06 is 719.45 thousand tonnes which increased to 801.36 thousand tonnes in 2010-11.

3.8.2 ESTIMATES OF POPULATION DISTRIBUTION BY AGE GROUPS

The estimated population distribution for the state of Karnataka by different age groups required for the projection of food grains requirement for the year 2006 and 2011 is shown in Fig. 3.15 and 3.16.

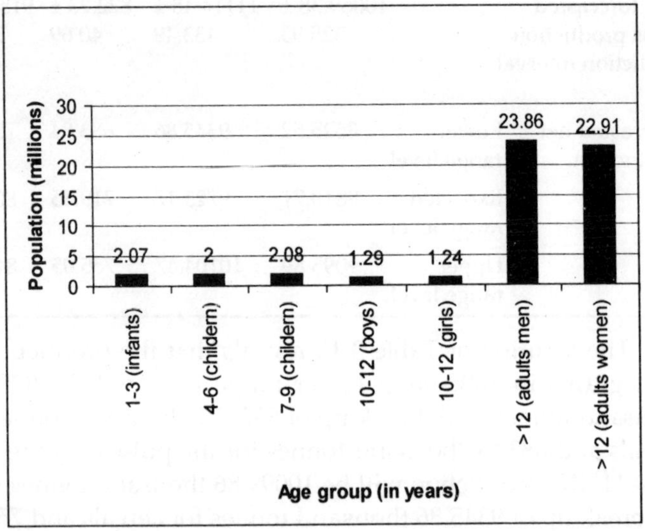

Fig. 3.15: Population distribution by age groups in 2006

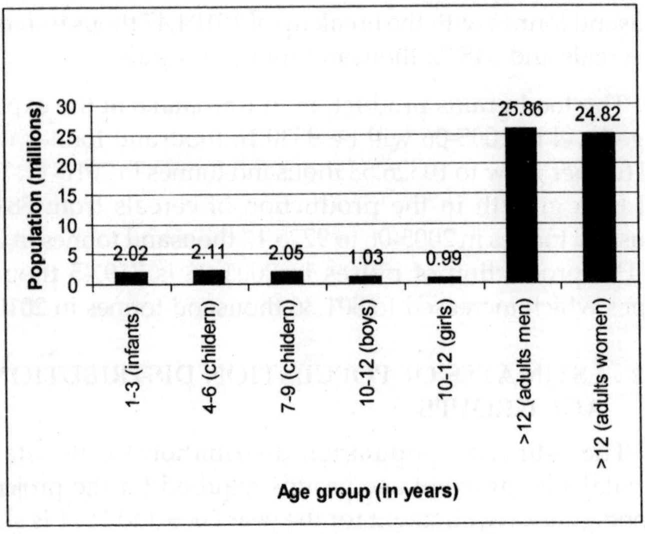

Fig. 3.16: Population distribution by age groups in 2011

3.8.3 PROJECTIONS OF FOOD GRAINS REQUIREMENT

The projections for food grain requirement by different age groups separately for cereals and pulses, on the basis of balanced diet has been estimated for the year 2006 and 2011 and the same is given in Table 3.16. On the basis of constructed population distribution by age groups and balanced diet recommendation for cereals and pulses, the estimated results show that the food grains requirement for the Karnataka state will be 11112.22 and 11854.72 thousand tonnes for the year 2006 and 2011 respectively.The break up will be 10083.00 and 10759.72 thousand tonnes for the cereals and 1029.22 and 1095.00 thousand tonnes of pulses for the two time periods. The requirement for food grains in 2006 by different age groups will be highest in adults (men) i.e. 5460.99 thousand tonnes followed by 4461.16 thousand tonnes for adults (women), 318.17 thousand tonnes for 7-9 years (children), 244.91 thousand tonnes for 4-6 years (children), 240.99 thousand tonnes for 10-12 years (boys), 211.45 thousand tonnes for 10-12 years (girls) and 174.55 thousand tonnes for 1-3 years (infants). By the year 2011, the food grains requirement will be highest in adults (men) i.e. 5917.53 thousand tonnes followed by 4833.68 thousand tonnes for adults (women), 313.59 thousand tonnes for 7-9 years (children), 192.41 thousand tonnes for 10-12 years (boys), 168.82 thousand tonnes for 10-12 years (girls), 258.38 thousand tonnes for 4-6 years (children) and 170.31 thousand tonnes for 1-3 years (infants).

Table 3.16. Forecasted requirement* for cereals and pulses by age groups in 2006 and 2011

(in thousand tonnes)

Food groups	*Cereals*		*Pulses*	
Year /Age groups	*2006*	*2011*	*2006*	*2011*
1-3 years	145.45 (132.23)	141.93 (129.03)	29.10 (26.45)	28.38 (25.80)

4-6 years		216.81 (197.10)	228.73 (207.94)	28.10 (25.54)	29.65 (26.95)
7-9 years		284.77 (258.88)	280.67 (255.15)	33.40 (30.36)	32.92 (29.92)
10-12 years	Boys	217.67 (197.88)	173.79 (157.99)	23.32 (21.20)	18.62 (16.92)
	Girls	189.06 (171.87)	150.95 (137.23)	22.39 (20.35)	17.87 (16.24)
Adults	Men	4981.96 (4529.05)	5398.45 (4907.68)	479.03 (435.48)	519.08 (471.89)
	Women	4047.28 (3679.34)	4385.20 (3986.54)	413.88 (376.25)	448.48 (407.71)
Total		10083.00 (9166.36)	10759.72 (9781.56)	1029.22 (935.65)	1095.00 (995.45)

*Forecasted requirement is at retail level.
Figure in parenthesis indicates the forecasted requirement at physiological level.

3.8.4 CONCLUSION

The estimates of food grains production and requirement indicated that overall cereals and pulses requirement would continue to be in deficit condition in both the periods. The total food grain deficit in 2005-06 will be 1582.06 thousand tonnes which increased to 1328.19 thousand tonnes in 2010-11. The net deficit of cereals in the state would be 1272.29 and 1034.55 thousand tonnes in 2005-06 and 2010-11. The net deficit of pulses in the state would be 309.77 and 293.64 thousand tonnes in the same periods. The per capita per day availability of food grains, excluding 0 years population age group, in the state in year 2005-06 will be 470.97 grams which decreased to 489.81 grams in 2010-11. The estimated per capita per day availability (excluding 0 years population age group) of cereals would be 435.42 and 452.52 grams for the year 2005-06 and 2010-11 while the per capita per day availability of pulses is 35.55 and 37.29 grams for the same time periods. The estimated ranges i.e. pessimistic range and optimistic range in which the per capita per day availability for cereals may vary is 421.24 to 449.42 grams and 434.87 to 470.17 grams for the year 2005-06 and 2010-11. The estimated limits for the pulses is 33.79 to 37.31 grams and 35.08 to 39.49 grams for the same periods.

3.9
KERALA

The state of Kerala has total geographical area of about 3,886 thousand hectares. The population of the state, as per census 2001, is 31,841,374, out of which about 26% of population resides in urban area. The sex ratio (i.e. females per thousand males) and population density (average number of persons per sq km) is 1,058 and 819 respectively. The total literacy rate in state is 90.90% which comprises 94.2% for male as against 87.7% for females. The state of Kerala is located in south India. It is bounded by Karnataka in north, east and south east by Tamil Nadu, south-west and west by the Indian Ocean.

Kerala is an Agrarian economy and cash crops, like coconuts, rubber, tea and coffee, pepper and cardamom, cashew, areca nut, nutmeg, ginger, cinnamon, cloves, give the agriculture of Kerala a distinct flavour. Paddy is a major food grain crop and has a share of about 11% of the total cropped area. It is coconut which bring the people their principal source of earning in agriculture. Nearly 70% of Indian output of coconuts is provided by Kerala. Cashew is an another important cash crop of the state. The state has facilities for converting raw cashew into the dried fruit, salted or plain. Cardamom is another cash crop which gives Kerala a distinctive place in Indian export.

3.9.1 PROJECTIONS OF FOOD GRAINS PRODUCTION

The projections of food grains separately for the cereals and pulses for the state of Kerala at lower (pessimistic), expected (normal) and upper (optimistic) level for the year 2005-06 and 2010-11 is presented in the Table 3.17.

Table 3.17: Forecasted production of cereals and pulses for the year 2005-06 and 2010-11.

(in thousand tonnes)

Crop groups		*Cereals*		*Pulses*	
Year /Production		*2005-06*	*2010-11*	*2005-06*	*2010-11*
Forecasted gross production		689.21	586.61	21.30	21.30
95% forecasted gross production prediction interval		689.21 ± 151.05	586.61± 213.23	21.30 ± 10.63	21.30 ± 15.72
Forecasted net production	Lower range level	470.89	326.70	9.33	4.88
	Expected range level	603.06	513.28	18.63	18.63
	Upper range level	735.21	699.86	27.93	32.39

The scrutiny of Table 3.17 reveals that the production of food grains in 2005-06 at lower range level will be 480.22 thousand tonnes with break up of thousand tonnes for cereals and 11.89 thousand tonnes for the pulses. By the year 2010-11, the production will be 1263.62 thousand tonnes with the break up of 1250.79 thousand tonnes for cereals and 12.83 thousand tonnes for pulses.

At upper range level, the production of food grains in 2005-06 will be 1531.34 thousand tonnes with break up of 1517.27 thousand tonnes for cereals and 14.07 thousand tonnes for pulses. By the year 2010-11, the production will be 1605.48 thousand tonnes with the break up of 1589.73 thousand tonnes for cereals and 15.75 thousand tonnes for pulses.

The forecast of the food grains production in at the expected range level in 2005-06 will be 1355.50 thousand tonnes which will further grow to 1434.55 thousand tonnes in 2010-11. The production of cereals increased from 1342.52 thousand tonnes in 2005-06 to 1420.26 thousand tonnes in 2010-11. The production of pulses increased from 14.07 thousand tonnes to 15.75 thousand tonnes in the same period.

3.9.2 ESTIMATES OF POPULATION DISTRIBUTION BY AGE GROUPS

The estimated population distribution for the state of Kerala by different age groups required for the projection of food grains requirement for the year 2006 and 2011 is shown in Fig. 3.17 and 3.18.

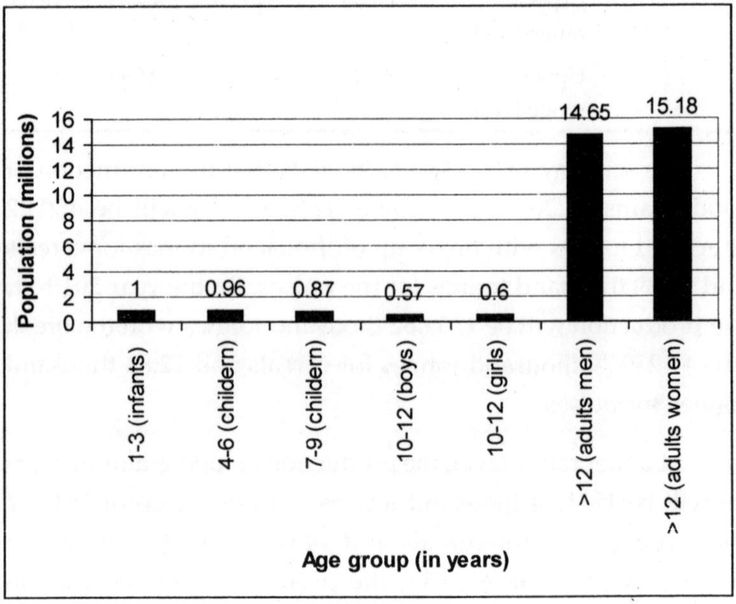

Fig. 3.17: Population distribution by age groups in 2006

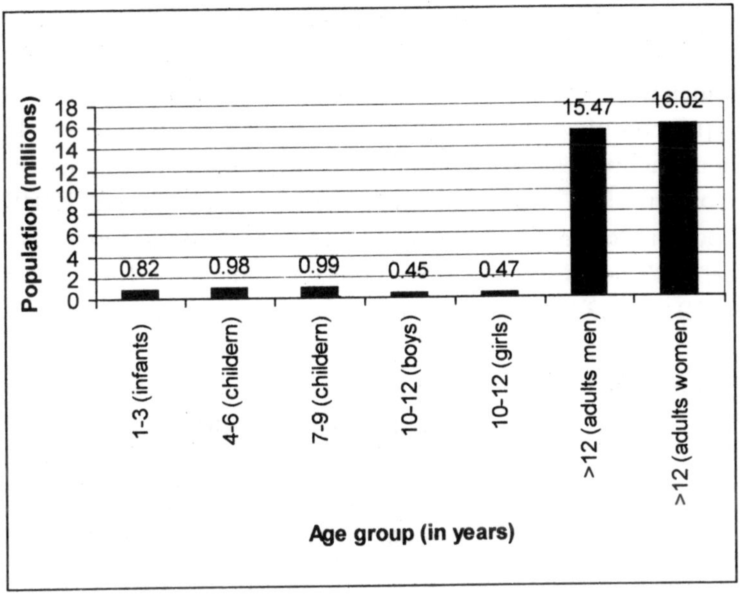

Fig. 3.18: Population distribution by age groups in 2011

3.9.3 PROJECTIONS OF FOOD GRAINS REQUIREMENT

The projections for food grain requirement by different age groups separately for cereals and pulses, on the basis of balanced diet has been estimated for the year 2006 and 2011 and the same is given in Table 3.18. On the basis of constructed population distribution by age groups and balanced diet recommendation for cereals and pulses, the estimated results show that the food grains requirement for the Kerala state will be 6852.58 and 7164.46 thousand tonnes for the year 2006 and 2011 respectively.The break up will be 6221.56 and 6506.69 thousand tonnes for the cereals and 631.02 and 657.77 thousand tonnes of pulses for the two time periods. The requirement for food grains in 2006 by different age groups will be highest in adults (men) i.e. 3353.02 thousand tonnes followed by 2955.71 thousand tonnes for adults (women), 133.09 thousand tonnes for 7-9 years children, 117.57 thousand tonnes for 4-6 years (children) 107.29 thousand tonnes for 10-12 years (boys), 101.58 thousand tonnes for 10-12 years (girls),and 84.32 thousand tonnes for 1-3 years (infants). By the year 2011, the food grains requirement will be highest in adults (men) i.e. 3539.47 thousand tonnes followed by 3120.19 thousand tonnes for adults (women), 151.43 thousand tonnes for 7-9 years (children), 120.01 thousand tonnes for 4-6 years (children) 84.36 thousand tonnes for 10-12 years (boys), 79.87 thousand tonnes for 10-12 years (girls) and 69.13 thousand tonnes for 1-3 years (infants).

Table 3.18. Forecasted requirement* for cereals and pulses by age groups in 2006 and 2011

(in thousand tonnes)

Crop groups		*Cereals*		*Pulses*	
Year/Production		*2005-06*	*2010-11*	*2005-06*	*2010-11*
1-3 years		70.26	57.61	14.06	11.52
		(63.87)	(52.37)	(12.78)	(10.47)
4-6 years		104.07	106.24	13.50	13.77
		(94.61)	(96.58)	(12.27)	(12.52)
7-9 years	119.12	135.54	13.97	15.89	
		(108.29)	(123.22)	(12.70)	(14.44)
10-12 years	Boys	96.91	76.20	10.38	8.16
		(88.10)	(69.27)	(9.44)	(7.42)
	Girls	90.83	71.42	10.75	8.45
		(82.57)	(64.93)	(9.77)	(7.68)
Adults	Men	3058.90	3228.99	294.12	310.48
		(2780.82)	(2935.44)	(267.38)	(282.25)
	Women	2681.47	2830.69	274.24	289.50
		(2437.70)	(2573.35)	(249.31)	(263.18)
Total		6221.56	6506.69	631.02	657.77
		(5655.96)	(5915.17)	(573.65)	(597.97)

*Forecasted requirement is at retail level.

Figure in parenthesis indicates the forecasted requirement at physiological level.

3.9.4 CONCLUSION

The estimates of food grains production and requirement indicated that overall cereals and pulses requirement would continue to be in deficit condition in both the periods. The total food grain deficit in 2005-06 will be 6230.89 thousand tonnes which increased to 6632.55 thousand tonnes in 2010-11. The net deficit of cereals in the state would be 5618.50 and 5993.41 thousand tonnes in 2005-06 and 2010-11. The net deficit of pulses in the state would be 612.39 and 639.14 thousand tonnes in the same periods. The per capita per day availability of food grains, excluding 0 years population age group, in the state in year 2005-06 will be 50.34 grams which decreased to 41.40 grams in 2010-11. The estimated per capita per day availability (excluding 0 years population age group) of cereals would be 48.84 and 39.95 grams for the year 2005-06 and 2010-11 while the per capita per day availability of pulses is 1.50 and 1.45 grams for the same time periods. The estimated ranges i.e. pessimistic range and optimistic range in which the per capita per day availability for cereals may vary is 38.13 to 59.54 grams and 25.43 to 54.47 grams for the year 2005-06 and 2010-11. The estimated limits for the pulses is 0.75 to 2.26 grams and 0.38 to 2.52 grams for the same periods.

3.10
MADHYA PRADESH

(The analysis in this section is pertaining to Undivided Madhya Pradesh)

The Madhya Pradesh is one of the major states of the Indian Union. On the 1st November, 2000, the new state Chattisgarh was carved out of Madhya Pradesh as 26th state of India. Now, after the formation of Chattishgarh, the Madhya Pradesh has total geographical area of about 30,800 thousand hectares with population of the state, as per census 2001, is 60,348,023 out of which about 26.5% of population resides in urban area. The sex ratio (i.e. females per thousand males) and population density (average number of persons per sq km) is 919 and 196 respectively. The total literacy rate in state is 63.7% which comprises 76.1% for male as against 50.3% for females. The state of Madhya Pradesh is situated in central India and surrounded by nine states. It is bounded by Rajasthan in the north-west, by Uttar Pradesh in the north, by Bihar and Jharkhand on the north-east, by Orissa and Chattisgarh on the east, by Andhra Pradesh and Maharashtra on the south and Gujarat in the west.

The State of Madhya Pradesh is primarily an agricultural state and it is the main stay of the state economy. Madhya Pradesh is predominantly Kharif crops growing state. In food grains, the major crops grown in the state are paddy, wheat, maize, jowar, gram, tur, urad and moong while soybean, groundnut and mustard among oilseeds. The introduction of soybean in the state during eighties, boost the oilseed production & thereby improvement in the economic condition of the farmers, as it fetches high prices. The commercial crops like cotton and sugarcane are also grown in considerable area in few districts. Medicinal and narcotic crops along with onion, garlic, and fruits like papaya, banana, oranges, mango and grapes are also grown in the state.

The newly formed Chattishgarh state has total geographical area of about 1,35,13 thousand hectares. The population of the state, as per census 2001, is 20,833,803, out of which about 20.1% of population resides in urban area. The sex ratio (i.e. females per thousand males) and population density (average number of persons per sq km) is 989 and 154 respectively. The total literacy rate in state is 64.7 which comprise 77.4% for male as against 51.9% for females.

Previously, Chattishgarh is known as the "rice bowl" of the undivided Madhya Pradesh, as this part used to produce about seventy percent of the total paddy production in the state. Chhatisgarh produced nearly half of all food grains and one third of all major food crops grown in the undivided Madhya Pradesh during the Kharif season. The main Rabi crops of Chattisgarh are jowar, gram, urad, moong and moth. In pulses, a quarter of all produce in Madhya Pradesh during the rabi season comes from Chattisgarh.

3.10.1 PROJECTIONS OF FOOD GRAINS PRODUCTION

The projections of food grains separately for the cereals and pulses for the state of Madhya Pradesh at lower (pessimistic), expected (normal) and upper (optimistic) level for the year 2005-06 and 2010-11 is presented in the Table 3.19.

Table 3.19: Forecasted production of cereals and pulses for the year 2005-06 and 2010-11.

(in thousand tonnes)

Crop groups		*Cereals*		*Pulses*	
Year/Production		*2005-06*	*2010-11*	*2005-06*	*2010-11*
Forecasted gross production		18560.38	20272.38	4166.01	4411.01
95% forecasted gross production prediction interval		18560.38 ± 544.21	20272.38 ± 723.81	4166.01 ± 107.86	4411.01 ± 143.43
Forecasted net production	Lower range level	15764.14	17105.00	3550.88	3734.11
	Expected range level	16240.33	17738.33	3645.26	3859.63
	Upper range level	16716.51	18371.66	3739.63	3985.13

The scrutiny of Table 3.19 reveals that the production of food grains in 2005-06 at lower range level will be 19315.02 thousand tonnes with break up of 15764.14 thousand tonnes for cereals and 3550.88 thousand tonnes for the pulses. By the year 2010-11, the production will be 20839.11 thousand tonnes with the break up of 17105.00 thousand tonnes for cereals and 3734.11 thousand tonnes for pulses.

At upper range level, the production of food grains in 2005-06 will be 20456.14 thousand tonnes with break up of 16716.51 thousand tonnes for cereals and 3739.63 thousand tonnes for pulses. By the year 2010-11, the production will be 22356.79 thousand tonnes with the break up 18371.66 thousand tonnes for cereals and 3985.13 thousand tonnes for pulses.

The food grains production in Madhya Pradesh at the expected range level in 2005-06 will be 19885.59 thousand tonnes which will further grow to 21597.96 thousand tonnes in 2010-11. There will be a growth in the production of cereals from 16240.33 thousand tonnes in 2005-06 to 17738.33 thousand tonnes in 2010-11. The production of pulses in 2005-06 is 3645.26 thousand tonnes which increased to 3859.63 thousand tonnes in 2010-11.

3.10.2 ESTIMATES OF POPULATION DISTRIBUTION BY AGE GROUPS

The estimated population distribution for the state of Madhya Pradesh by different age groups required for the projection of food grains requirement for the year 2006 and 2011is shown in Fig. 3.19 and 3.20.

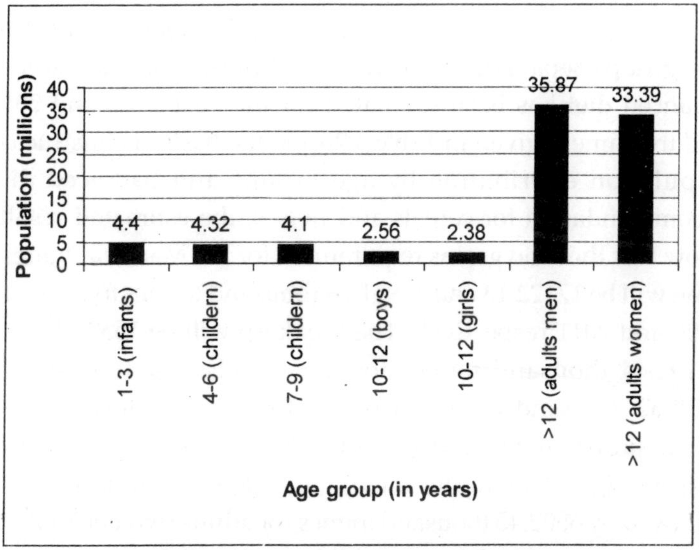

Fig. 3.19: Population distribution by age groups in 2006

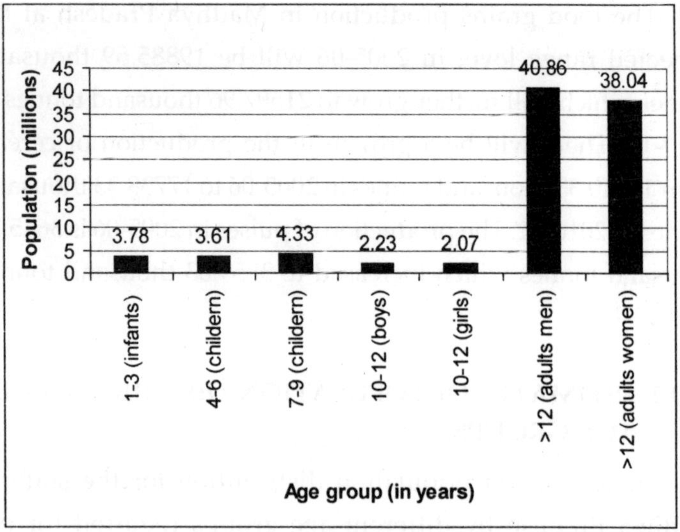

Fig. 3.20: Population distribution by age groups in 2011

3.10.3 PROJECTIONS OF FOOD GRAINS REQUIREMENT

The projections for food grain requirement by different age groups separately for cereals and pulses, on the basis of balanced diet has been estimated for the year 2006 and 2011 and the same is given in Table 3.20. On the basis of constructed population distribution by age groups and balanced diet recommendation for cereals and pulses, the estimated results show that the food grains requirement for the Madhya Pradesh state will be 17122.13 and 18951.06 thousand tonnes for the year 2006 and 2011 respectively.The break up will be 15521.12 and 17192.44 thousand tonnes for the cereals and 1601.01 and 1758.62 thousand tonnes of pulses for the two time periods. The requirement for food grains in 2006 by different age groups will be highest in adults (men) i.e. 8208.44 thousand tonnes followed by 6502.45 thousand tonnes for adults (women), 627.19 thousand tonnes for 7-9 years (children), 529.02 thousand tonnes for 4-6 years (children), 477.62 thousand tonnes for 10-12 years (boys), 406.41 thousand tonnes for 10-12 years (girls) and 371.00 thousand tonnes for 1-3 years (infants). By the year 2011, the food grains requirement will be highest in adults (men) i.e.9350.93 thousand tonnes followed by 7407.49 thousand tonnes for adults (women), 662.36 thousand tonnes for 7-9 years (children), 442.07 thousand tonnes for 4-6 years (children), 415.74 thousand tonnes for 10-12 years (boys), 353.76 thousand tonnes for 10-12 years (girls) and 318.71 thousand tonnes for 1-3 years (infants).

Table 3.20. Forecasted requirement* for cereals and pulses by age groups in 2006 and 2011

(in thousand tonnes)

Food groups		*Cereals*		*Pulses*	
Year/Age groups		*2006*	*2011*	*2006*	*2011*
1-3 years		309.16 (281.05)	265.59 (241.44)	61.84 (56.22)	53.12 (48.29)
4-6 years		468.31 (425.74)	391.34 (355.76)	60.71 (55.19)	50.73 (46.12)
7-9 years		561.34 (510.31)	592.82 (538.93)	65.85 (59.86)	69.54 (63.22)
10-12 years	Boys	431.40 (392.18)	375.51 (341.37)	46.22 (42.02)	40.23 (36.57)
	Girls	363.38 (330.34)	316.30 (287.54)	43.03 (39.12)	37.46 (34.05)
Adults	Men	7488.40 (6807.64)	8530.68 (7755.16)	720.04 (654.58)	820.25 (745.68)
	Women	5899.13 (5362.84)	6720.20 (6109.27)	603.32 (548.47)	687.29 (624.81)
Total		15521.12 (14110.11)	17192.44 (15629.48)	1601.01 (1455.46)	1758.62 (1598.74)

*Forecasted requirement is at retail level.

Figure in parenthesis indicates the forecasted requirement at physiological level.

3.10.4 CONCLUSION

The estimates of food grains production and requirement indicated that overall cereals and pulses requirement would continue to be in surplus in both the periods. The total food grains surplus in 2005-06 will be 2763.46 thousand tonnes which increased to 2646.90 thousand tonnes in 2010-11. The net surplus of cereals in the state would be 719.21 and 545.89 thousand tonnes in 2005-06 and 2010-11. The net surplus of pulses in the state would be 2044.25 and 2101.01 thousand tonnes in the same periods. The per capita per day availability of food grains, excluding 0 years population age group, in the state in year 2005-06 will be 626.07 grams which decreased to 623.39 grams in 2010-11. The estimated per capita per day availability (excluding 0 years population age group) of cereals would be 511.31 and 511.99 grams for the year 2005-06 and 2010-11 while the per capita per day availability of pulses is 114.76 and 111.40 grams for the same time periods. The estimated ranges i.e. pessimistic range and optimistic range in which the per capita per day availability for cereals may vary is 496.31 to 526.30 grams and 493.71 to 530.27 grams for the year 2005-06 and 2010-11. The estimated limits for the pulses are 111.79 to 117.74 grams and 107.78 to 115.02 grams for the same periods.

3.11
MAHARASHTRA

The state of Maharashtra has total geographical area of about 30,776 thousand hectares. The population of the state, as per census 2001, is 96,878,627 out of which about 42.4% of population resides in urban area. The sex ratio (i.e. females per thousand males) and population density (average number of persons per sq km) is 922 and 315 respectively. The total literacy rate in state is 76.9% which comprises 86.0% for male as against 67.0% for females.

The state of Maharashtra is located in central India. It is bounded north and east by Madhya Pradesh, south by Andhra Pradesh, Karnataka and Goa, west by the Arabian sea and north west by Daman and Gujrat. The principal food grains crops grown in the state are rice, jowar, bajra, wheat, mung, urd, gram and other pulses. About 65% of the total workers in the state depend on agriculture and allied activities.

3.11.1 PROJECTIONS OF FOOD GRAINS PRODUCTION

The projections of food grains separately for the cereals and pulses for the state of Maharahtra at lower (pessimistic), expected (normal) and upper (optimistic) level for the year 2005-06 and 2010-11 is presented in the Table 3.21.

Table 3.21: Forecasted production of cereals and pulses for the year 2005-06 and 2010-11

(in thousand tonnes)

Crop groups	*Cereals*		*Pulses*	
Year /Production	*2005-06*	*2010-11*	*2005-06*	*2010-11*
Forecasted gross production	12443.40	13410.90	2460.46	2775.91

95% forecasted gross production prediction interval		12443.40 ± 880.83	13410.90 ± 1171.51	2460.46 ± 177.07	2775.91 ± 269.09
Forecasted net production	Lower range level	10117.25	10709.47	1997.96	2193.47
	Expected range level	10887. 97	11734.54	2152.90	2428.92
	Upper range level	11658.70	12759.61	2307.84	2664.37

The scrutiny of Table 3.21 reveals that the production of food grains in 2005-06 at lower range level will be 12115.21 thousand tonnes with break up of 10117.25 thousand tonnes for cereals and 1997.96 thousand tonnes for the pulses. By the year 2010-11, the production will be 12902.94 thousand tonnes with the break up of 10709.47 thousand tonnes for cereals and 2193.47 thousand tonnes for pulses.

At upper range level, the production of food grains in 2005-06 will be 13966.54 thousand tonnes with break up of 11658.70 thousand tonnes for cereals and 2307.84 thousand tonnes for pulses. By the year 2010-11, the production will be 15423.98 thousand tonnes with the break up 12759.61 thousand tonnes for cereals and 2664.37 thousand tonnes for pulses.

The forecast of the food grains production in Maharashtra at the expected range level in 2005-06 will be 13040.87 thousand tonnes which will further grow to 14163.46 thousand tonnes in 2010-11. There will be a growth in the production of cereals from 10887.97 thousand tonnes in 2005-06 to 11734.54 thousand tonnes in 2010-11. The production of pulses in 2005-06 is 2152.90 thousand tonnes which increased to 2428.92 thousand tonnes in 2010-11.

3.11.2 ESTIMATES OF POPULATION DISTRIBUTION BY AGE GROUPS

The estimated population distribution for the state of Maharahtra by different age groups required for the projection of food grains requirement for the year 2006 and 2011 is shown in Fig. 3.21 and 3.22.

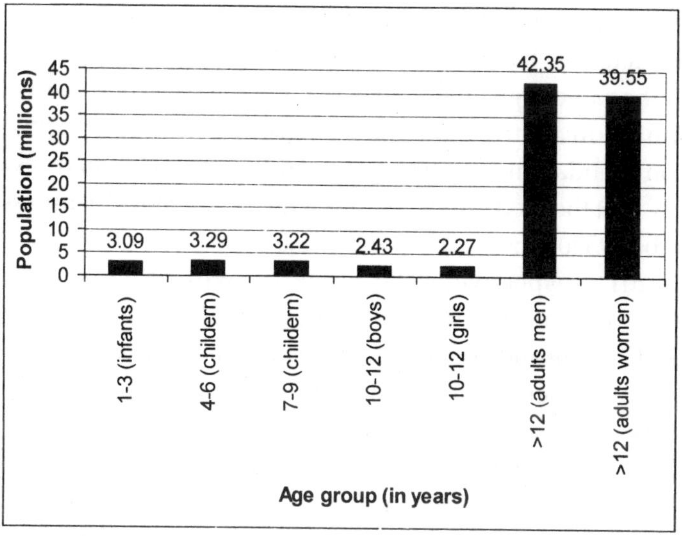

Fig. 3.21: Population distribution by age groups in 2006

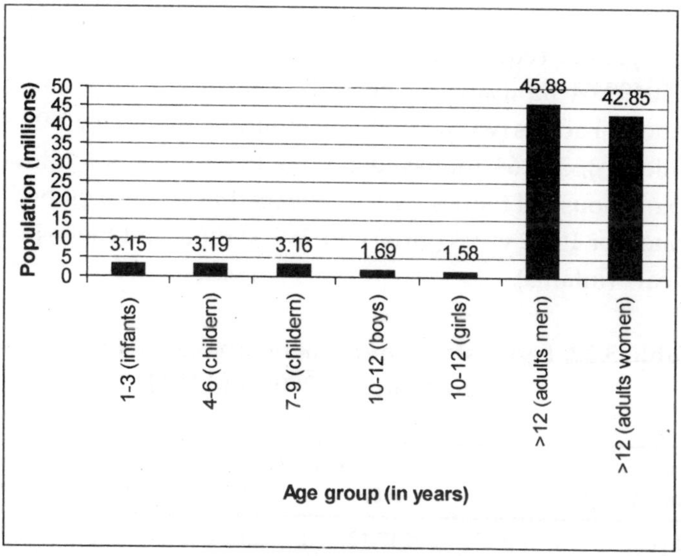

Fig. 3.22: Population distribution by age groups in 2011

3.11.3 PROJECTIONS OF FOOD GRAINS REQUIREMENT

The projections for food grain requirement by different age groups separately for cereals and pulses, on the basis of balanced diet has been estimated for the year 2006 and 2011 and the same is given in Table 3.22. On the basis of constructed population distribution by age groups and balanced diet recommendation for cereals and pulses, the estimated results show that the food grains requirement for the Maharashtra state will be 19390.35 and 20568.66 thousand tonnes for the year 2006 and 2011 respectively.The break up will be 17599.38 and 18674.51 thousand tonnes for the cereals and 1790.97 and 1894.15 thousand tonnes of pulses for the two time periods. The requirement for food grains in 2006 by different age groups will be highest in adults (men) i.e. 9691.42 thousand tonnes followed by 7701.92 thousand tonnes for adults (women), 492.56 thousand tonnes for 7-9 years (children), 402.88 thousand tonnes for 4-6 years (children), 453.71 thousand tonnes for 10-12 years (boys), 387.32 thousand tonnes for 10-12 years (girls) and 260.54 thousand tonnes for 1-3 years (infants). By the year 2011, the food grains requirement will be highest in adults (men) i.e.10499.64 thousand tonnes followed by 8344.26 thousand tonnes for adults (women), 483.39 thousand tonnes for 7-9 years (children), 390.64 thousand tonnes for 4-6 years (children), 315.67 thousand tonnes for 10-12 years (boys), 269.47 thousand tonnes for 10-12 years (girls) and 265.58 thousand tonnes for 1-3 years (infants).

Table 3.22. Forecasted requirement* for cereals and pulses by age groups in 2006 and 2011

(in thousand tonnes)

Food groups	*Cereals*		*Pulses*	
Year /Age groups	*2006*	*2011*	*2006*	*2011*
1-3 years	217.12 (197.38)	221.32 (201.20)	43.42 (39.47)	44.26 (40.24)

4-6 years		356.65 (324.23)	345.81 (314.37)	46.23 (42.03)	44.83 (40.75)
7-9 years		440.85 (400.77)	432.64 (393.31)	51.71 (47.01)	50.75 (46.14)
10-12 years	Boys	409.80 (372.54)	285.12 (259.20)	43.91 (39.92)	30.55 (27.77)
	Girls	346.31 (314.83)	240.94 (219.04)	41.01 (37.28)	28.53 (25.94)
Adults	Men	8841.30 (8037.54)	9578.62 (8707.84)	850.12 (772.84)	921.02 (837.29)
	Women	6987.35 (6352.14)	7570.05 (6881.86)	714.57 (649.61)	774.21 (703.83)
Total		17599.38 (15999.44)	18674.51 (16976.83)	1790.97 (1628.15)	1894.15 (1721.95)

*Forecasted requirement is at retail level.

Figure in parenthesis indicates the forecasted requirement at physiological level.

3.11.4 CONCLUSION

The estimates of food grains production and requirement indicated that cereals requirement would be in deficit condition in 2005-06 while pulses requirement would surplus in both the periods. The net deficit of cereals in the state would be 6711.41 and 6939.97 thousand tonnes in 2005-06 and 2010-11. The net surplus of pulses in the state would be 361.93 thousand tonnes in the year 2005-06 and 534.77 thousand tonnes in 2010-11. The per capita per day availability of food grains, excluding 0 years population age group, in the state in year 2005-06 will be 371.39 grams which increased to382.30 grams in 2010-11. The estimated per capita per day availability (excluding 0 years population age group) of cereals would be 310.08 and 316.74 grams for the year 2005-06 and 2010-11 while the per capita per day availability of pulses is 61.31 and 65.56 grams for the same time periods. The estimated ranges i.e. pessimistic range and optimistic range in which the per capita per day availability for cereals may vary is 288.13 to 332.03 grams and 289.07 to 344.41 grams for the year 2005-06 and 2010-11. The estimated limits for the pulses are 56.90 to 65.72 grams and 59.21 to 71.92 grams for the same periods.

3.12
ORISSA

The state of Orissa has total geographical area of about 15,584 thousand hectares which may be divided into four regions-the northern plateau, central river basin, eastern hills and coastal plains.

The population of the state, as per census 2001, is 36,804,660 out of which about 15.0% of population resides in urban area. The sex ratio (i.e. females per thousand males) and population density (average number of persons per sq km) is 972 and 236 respectively. The total literacy rate in state is 63.1% which comprises 75.3% for male as against 50.5% for females. The state of Orissa is situated in the north-eastern part of Indian peninsula and is bounded by the Bay of Bengal in the east, West Bengal in the north-east, Bihar in the north, Madhya Pradesh in the west and Andhra Pradesh in the south.

Like most of the states of the country, the economy of Orissa is also determined by agriculture. The rice and sugarcane is the main cereal and cash crop respectively, in the state.

3.12.1 PROJECTIONS OF FOOD GRAINS PRODUCTION

The projections of food grains separately for the cereals and pulses for the state of Orissa at lower (pessimistic), expected (normal) and upper (optimistic) level for the year 2005-06 and 2010-11 is presented in the Table 3.23.

Table 3.23: Forecasted production of cereals and pulses for the year 2005-06 and 2010-11

(in thousand tonnes)

Crop groups	*Cereals*		*Pulses*	
Year /Production	*2005-06*	*2010-11*	*2005-06*	*2010-11*
Forecasted gross production	6300.00	6475.33	323.78	323.78

95% forecasted gross production prediction interval		6300.00 ± 1078.07	6475.33 ± 1087.88	323.78 ± 122.57	323.78 ± 122.57
Forecasted net production	Lower range level	4569.18	4714.02	176.06	176.06
	Expected range level	5512.50	5665.91	283.31	283.31
	Upper range level	6455.81	6617.81	390.55	390.55

The scrutiny of Table 3.23 reveals that the production of food grains in 2005-06 at lower range level will be 4745.24 thousand tonnes with break up of 4569.18 thousand tonnes for cereals and 176.06 thousand tonnes for the pulses. By the year 2010-11, the production will be 4890.08 thousand tonnes with the break up of 4714.02 thousand tonnes for cereals and 176.06 thousand tonnes for pulses.

At upper range level, the production of food grains in 2005-06 will be 6846.36 thousand tonnes with break up of 6455.81 thousand tonnes for cereals and 390.55 and tonnes for pulses. By the year 2010-11, the production will be thousand tonnes with the break up of 6617.81 thousand tonnes for cereals and 390.55 thousand tonnes for pulses.

The food grains production in Orissa at the expected range level in 2005-06 will be 5795.81 thousand tonnes which will further grow to 5949.22 thousand tonnes in 2010-11. The production of cereals increased from 5512.50 thousand tonnes in 2005-06 to 5665.91 thousand tonnes in 2010-11. The production of pulses in 2005-06 is 283.31 which remained stagnant in 2010-11.

3.12.2 ESTIMATES OF POPULATION DISTRIBUTION BY AGE GROUPS

The estimated population distribution for the state of Orissa by different age groups required for the projection of food grains requirement for the year 2006 and 2011 is shown in Fig. 3.23 and 3.24.

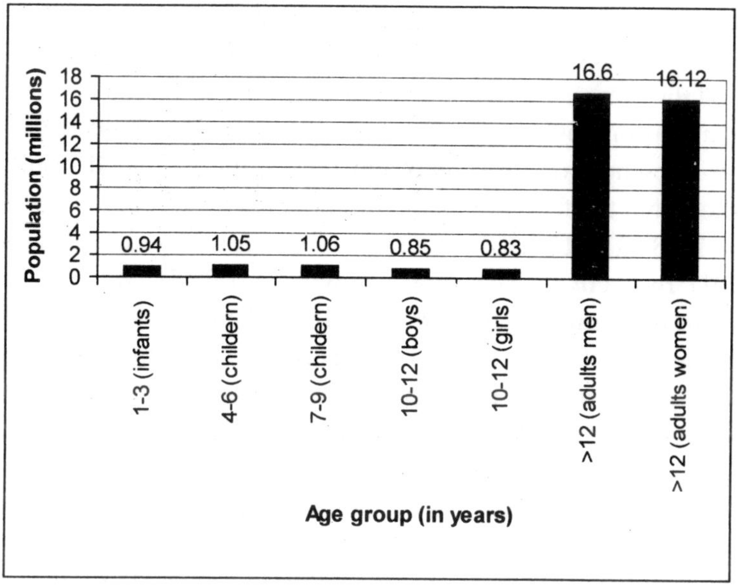

Fig. 3.23: Population distribution by age groups in 2006

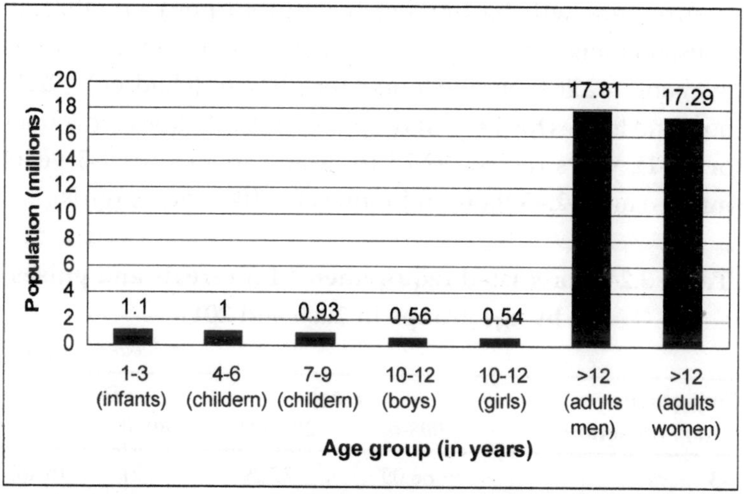

Fig. 3.24: Population distribution by age groups in 2011

3.12.3 PROJECTIONS OF FOOD GRAINS REQUIREMENT

The projections for food grain requirement by different age groups separately for cereals and pulses, on the basis of balanced diet has been estimated for the year 2006 and 2011 and the same is given in Table 3.24. On the basis of constructed population distribution by age groups and balanced diet recommendation for cereals and pulses, the estimated results show that the food grains requirement for the Orissa state will be 7608.25 and 7996.80 thousand tonnes for the year 2006 and 2011 respectively.The break up will be 6908.51 and 7262.56 thousand tonnes for the cereals and 699.74 and 734.24 thousand tonnes of pulses for the two time periods. The requirement for food grains in 2006 by different age groups will be highest in adults (men) i.e. 3799.15 thousand tonnes followed by 3138.86 thousand tonnes for adults (women), 162.14 thousand tonnes for 7-9 years children, 159.05 thousand tonnes for 10-12 years (boys), 141.22 thousand tonnes for 10-12 years (girls), 128.57 thousand tonnes for 4-6 years (children) and 79.26 thousand tonnes for 1-3 years (infants). By the year 2011, the food grains requirement will be highest in adults (men) i.e. 4075.49 thousand tonnes followed by 3367.18 thousand tonnes for adults (women), 142.26 thousand tonnes for 7-9 years (children), 122.45 thousand tonnes for 4-6 years (children), 104.19 thousand tonnes for 10-12 years (boys), 92.75 thousand tonnes for 1-3 years (infants) and 92.48 thousand tonnes for 10-12 years (girls).

Table 3.24. Forecasted requirement* for cereals and pulses by age groups in 2006 and 2011

(in thousand tonnes)

Crop groups	*Cereals*		*Pulses*	
Year /Production	*2005-06*	*2010-11*	*2005-06*	*2010-11*
1-3 years	66.05 (60.04)	77.29 (70.26)	13.21 (12.00)	15.46 (14.05)

4-6 years		113.82 (103.47)	108.40 (98.54)	14.75 (13.41)	14.05 (12.77)
7-9 years		145.12 (131.93)	127.33 (115.75)	17.02 (15.47)	14.93 (13.57)
10-12 years	Boys	143.73 (130.66)	94.11 (85.55)	15.32 (13.23)	10.08 (9.16)
Girls		126.27 (114.79)	82.68 (75.16)	14.95 (13.59)	9.80 (8.90)
Adults	Men	3465.89 (3150.81)	3717.99 (3379.99)	333.26 (302.96)	357.50 (325.00)
Women		2847.63 (2588.75)	3054.76 (2777.05)	291.23 (264.75)	312.42 (284.02)
Total		6908.51 (6280.46)	7262.56 (6602.33)	699.74 (636.13)	734.24 (667.49)

*Forecasted requirement is at retail level.
Figure in parenthesis indicates the forecasted requirement at physiological level.

3.12.4 CONCLUSION

The estimates of food grains production and requirement indicated that overall cereals and pulses requirement would continue to be in deficit condition in both the periods. The total food grain deficit in 2005-06 will be 1812.44 thousand tonnes which increased to 2047.58 thousand tonnes in 2010-11. The net deficit of cereals in the state would be 1396.01 and 1596.65 thousand tonnes in 2005-06 and 2010-11. The net deficit of pulses in the state would be 416.43 and 450.93 thousand tonnes in the same periods. The per capita per day availability of food grains, excluding 0 years population age group, in the state in year 2005-06 will be 424.00 grams which decreased to 415.47 grams in 2010-11. The estimated per capita per day availability (excluding 0 years population age group) of cereals would be 403.28 and 395.69 grams for the year 2005-06 and 2010-11 while the per capita per day availability of pulses is 20.72 and 19.78 grams for the same time periods. The estimated ranges i.e. pessimistic range and optimistic range in which the per capita per day availability for cereals may vary is 334.27 to 472.28 grams and 329.21 to 462.17 grams for the year 2005-06 and 2010-11. The estimated limits for the pulses are 12.88 to 28.57 grams and 12.29 to 27.27 grams for the same periods.

3.13
PUNJAB

The state of Punjab has total geographical area of about 5,036 thousand hectares. The population of the state, as per census 2001, is 24,358,999, out of which about 33.9% of population resides in urban area. The sex ratio (i.e. females per thousand males) and population density (average number of persons per sq km) is 876 and 484 respectively. The total literacy rate in state is 69.7% which comprises 75.2% for male as against 63.4% for females. The state is situated in the northwest of India and is bordered by Pakistan on the west, the Indian states of Jammu and Kashmir on the north, Himachal Pradesh on its northeast and Haryana and Rajasthan to its south.

Punjab is the leading state in agricultural production in India. The state produces about 20% of India's wheat, 9% of the country's rice and 15% of the national output of cotton. This was achieved despite the fact that the state has only 1.6% of India's geographical area. At present over 84% of the total geographical area of the state stands cultivated. The cropping pattern is dominated by wheat crop and other major crops are rice, maize, gram, pulses, cotton and sugarcane.

3.13.1 PROJECTIONS OF FOOD GRAINS PRODUCTION

The projections of food grains separately for the cereals and pulses for the state of Punjab at lower (pessimistic), expected (normal) and upper (optimistic) level for the year 2005-06 and 2010-11 is presented in the Table 3.25.

Table 3.25: Forecasted production of cereals and pulses for the year 2005-06 and 2010-11

(in thousand tonnes)

Crop groups		*Cereals*		*Pulses*	
Year /Production		*2005-06*	*2010-11*	*2005-06*	*2010-11*
Forecasted gross production		25808.55	28148.55	28.55	18.82
95% forecasted gross production prediction interval		25808.55 ± 421.39	28148.55 ± 560.48	28.55 ± 15.46	18.82 ± 16.22
Forecasted net production	Lower range level	22213.76	24139.56	11.45	2.27
	Expected range level	22582.48	24629.98	24.98	16.47
	Upper range level	22951.20	25120.40	38.51	30.66

The scrutiny of Table 3.25 reveals that the production of food grains in 2005-06 at lower range level will be 22225.21 thousand tonnes with break up of 22213.76 thousand tonnes for cereals and 11.45 thousand tonnes for the pulses. By the year 2010-11, the production will be 24141.83 thousand tonnes with the break up of 24139.56 thousand tonnes for cereals and 2.27 thousand tonnes for pulses.

At upper range level, the production of food grains in 2005-06 will be 22989.71 thousand tonnes with break up of 22951.20 thousand tonnes for cereals and 38.51 thousand tonnes for pulses. By the year 2010-11, the production will be 25251.06 thousand tonnes with the break up 25120.40 thousand tonnes for cereals and 30.66 thousand tonnes for pulses.

The forecast of the food grains production in Punjab at the expected range level in 2005-06 will be 22607.46 thousand tonnes which will further grow to 24646.45 thousand tonnes in 2010-11. There will be a growth in the production of cereals from 22582.48 thousand tonnes in 2005-06 to 24629.98 thousand tonnes in 2010-11. The production of pulses in 2005-06 is 24.98 thousand tonnes which decreased to 16.47 thousand tonnes in 2010-11.

3.13.2 ESTIMATES OF POPULATION DISTRIBUTION BY AGE GROUPS

The estimated population distribution for the state of Punjab by different age groups required for the projection of food grains requirement for the year 2006 and 2011is shown in Fig. 3.25 and 3.26.

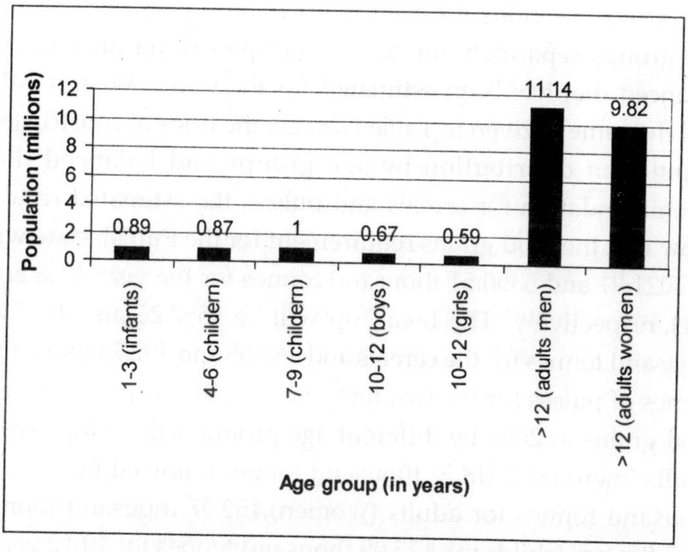

Fig. 3.25: Population distribution by age groups in 2006

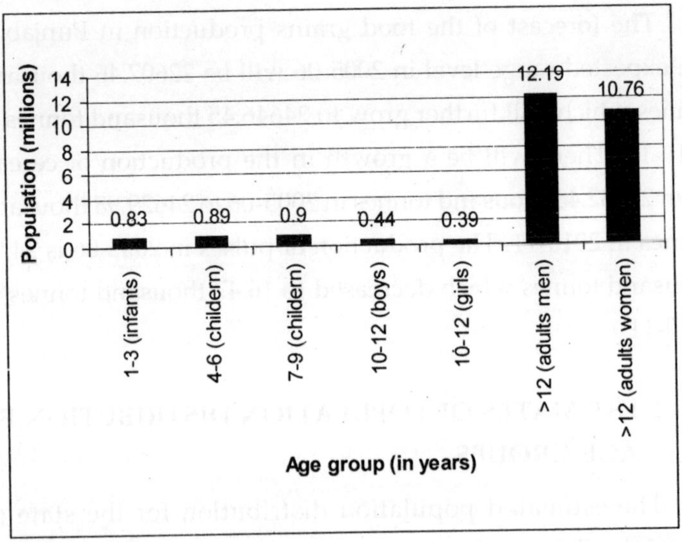

Fig. 3.26: Population distribution by age groups in 2011

3.13.3 PROJECTIONS OF FOOD GRAINS REQUIREMENT

The projections for food grain requirement by different age groups separately for cereals and pulses, on the basis of balanced diet has been estimated for the year 2006 and 2011 and the same is given in Table 3.26. On the basis of constructed population distribution by age groups and balanced diet recommendation for cereals and pulses, the estimated results show that the food grains requirement for the Punjab state will be 5021.91 and 5350.51 thousand tonnes for the year 2006 and 2011 respectively. The break up will be 4557.26 and 4857.77 thousand tonnes for the cereals and 464.65 and 492.74 thousand tonnes of pulses for the two time periods. The requirement for food grains in 2006 by different age groups will be highest in adults (men) i.e. 2548.77 thousand tonnes followed by 1912.73 thousand tonnes for adults (women),152.97 thousand tonnes for 7-9 years (children), 125.09 thousand tonnes for 10-12 years (boys), 106.53 thousand tonnes for 4-6 years (children), 100.77

thousand tonnes for 10-12 years (girls) and 75.04 thousand tonnes for 1-3 years (infants). By the year 2011, the food grains requirement will be highest in adults (men) i.e.2790.76 thousand tonnes followed by 2094.39 thousand tonnes for adults (women), 137.67 thousand tonnes for 7-9 years (children), 108.99 thousand tonnes for 4-6 years (children), 82.34 thousand tonnes for 10-12 years (boys), 69.98 thousand tonnes for 1-3 years (infants) and 66.36 thousand tonnes for 10-12 years (girls).

Table 3.26. Forecasted requirement* for cereals and pulses by age groups in 2006 and 2011

(in thousand tonnes)

Food groups		*Cereals*		*Pulses*	
Year/Age groups		*2006*	*2011*	*2006*	*2011*
1-3 years		62.53 (56.84)	58.32 (53.02)	12.51 (11.37)	11.66 (10.60)
4-6 years		94.31 (85.74)	96.48 (87.71)	12.22 (11.11)	12.51 (11.37)
7-9 years		136.91 (124.46)	123.22 (112.02)	16.06 (14.60)	14.45 (13.14)
10-12 years	Boys	112.89 (102.63)	74.37 (67.61)	12.20 (11.09)	7.97 (7.24)
	Girls	90.10 (81.91)	59.34 (53.94)	10.67 (9.7)	7.02 (6.38)
Adults	Men	2325.20 (2113.82)	2545.96 (2314.51)	223.57 (203.24)	244.80 (222.54)
	Women	1735.31 (1577.55)	1900.07 (172.34)	177.42 (161.29)	194.32 (176.65)
Total		4557.26 (4142.96)	4857.77 (4416.15)	464.65 (422.41)	492.74 (447.94)

*Forecasted requirement is at retail level.

Figure in parenthesis indicates the forecasted requirement at physiological level.

3.13.4 CONCLUSION

It is observed that the state of Punjab has a wide role to provide the food security to the nation. The estimates of food grains production and requirement indicated that overall there will be large surplus in case of cereals while the pulses requirement will continue to be in deficit condition. The net surplus of cereals available in the state will be 18025.22 and 19772.21 thousand tonnes in the year 2005-06 and 2010-11 while the deficit of pulses will be 439.67 and 476.27 thousand tonnes in the same periods.

The estimated per capita per day availability of food grains, excluding 0 years population age group, in the state in year 2005-06 will be 2479.51 grams which decreased to 2557.75 grams in 2010-11. The estimated per capita per day availability (excluding 0 years population age group) of cereals would be 2476.77 and 2556.04 grams for the year 2005-06 and 2010-11 while the per capita per day availability of pulses is 2.74 and 1.71 grams for the same time periods. The estimated ranges i.e. pessimistic range and optimistic range in which the per capita per day availability for cereals may vary is 2436.33 to 2517.21 grams and 405.14 to 2606.93 grams for the year 2005-06 and 2010-11. The estimated limits for the pulses are 1.25 to 4.22 grams and 0.24 to 3.18 grams for the same periods.

3.14
RAJASTHAN

The state of Rajasthan has total geographical area of about 34,222 thousand hectares. The population of the state, as per census 2001, is 56,507,188 out of which about 23.4% of population resides in urban area. The sex ratio (i.e. females per thousand males) and population density (average number of persons per sq km) is 921 and 165 respectively. The total literacy rate in state is 60.4% which comprises 75.7% for male as against 43.9% for females.The state of Rajasthan is located in north-west India. It is bounded north by Punjab, north east by Haryana and Uttar Pradesh, east by Madhya Pradesh, south by Gujarat and west by Pakistan.

Rajasthan is a predominantly agrarian state and principal crops cultivated in the state are rice, barley, jowar, millet, maize, gram, wheat, oilseeds and tobacco. The state has emerged as a leading oilseed producer in case of rapeseed, soybean and mustard.

3.14.1 PROJECTIONS OF FOOD GRAINS PRODUCTION

The projections of food grains separately for the cereals and pulses for the state of Rajasthan at lower (pessimistic), expected (normal) and upper (optimistic) level for the year 2005-06 and 2010-11 is presented in the Table 3.27.

Table 3.27: Forecasted production of cereals and pulses for the year 2005-06 and 2010-11

(in thousand tonnes)

Crop groups	*Cereals*		*Pulses*	
Year /Production	*2005-06*	*2010-11*	*2005-06*	*2010-11*
Forecasted gross production	14196.14	18245.08	2606.57	2993.27

95% forecasted gross production prediction interval		14196.14 ± 1624.92	18245.08 ± 1862.44	2606.57 ± 251.2	2993.27 ± 334.10
Forecasted net production	Lower range level	10999.82	14334.81	2060.95	2326.77
	Expected range level	12421.62	15964.44	2280.75	2619.11
	Upper range level	13843.43	17594.08	2500.55	2911.45

The scrutiny of Table 3.27 reveals that the production of food grains in 2005-06 at lower range level will be 13060.77 thousand tonnes with break up of 10999.82 thousand tonnes for cereals and 2060.95 thousand tonnes for the pulses. By the year 2010-11, the production will be 16660.81 thousand tonnes with the break up of 14334.81 thousand tonnes for cereals and 2326.77 thousand tonnes for pulses.

At upper range level, the production of food grains in 2005-06 will be 16343.98 thousand tonnes with break up of 13843.43 thousand tonnes for cereals and 2500.55 thousand tonnes for pulses. By the year 2010-11, the production will be 20505.53 thousand tonnes with the break up of 17594.08 thousand tonnes for cereals and 2911.45 thousand tonnes for pulses.

The food grains production in Rajasthan at the expected range level in 2005-06 will be 14702.37 thousand tonnes which will further grow to 18583.55 thousand tonnes in 2010-11. There will be a phenomenal growth in the state in the production of cereals from 12421.62 thousand tonnes in 2005-06 to 15964.44 thousand tonnes in 2010-11. The production of pulses in 2005-06 is 2280.75 thousand tonnes and increased to 2911.45 thousand tonnes in 2010-11.

3.14.2 ESTIMATES OF POPULATION DISTRIBUTION BY AGE GROUPS

The estimated population distribution for the state of Rajasthan by different age groups required for the projection of food grains requirement for the year 2006 and 2011is shown in Fig. 3.27 and 3.28.

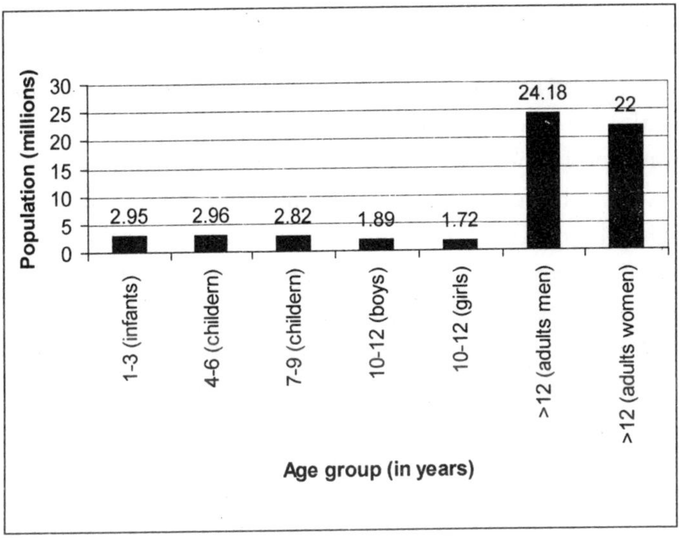

Fig. 3.27: Population distribution by age groups in 2006

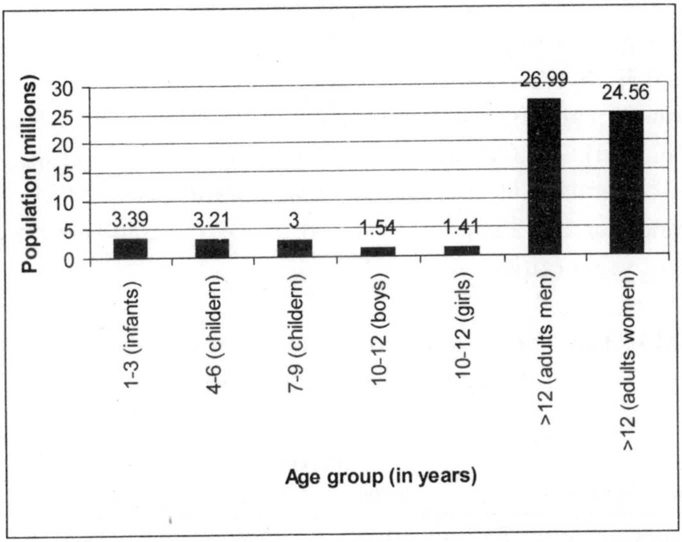

Fig. 3.28: Population distribution by age groups in 2011

3.14.3 PROJECTIONS OF FOOD GRAINS REQUIREMENT

The projections for food grain requirement by different age groups separately for cereals and pulses, on the basis of balanced diet has been estimated for the year 2006 and 2011 and the same is given in Table 3.28. On the basis of constructed population distribution by age groups and balanced diet recommendation for cereals and pulses, the estimated results show that the food grains requirement for the Rajasthan state will be 11506.64 and 12625.15 thousand tonnes for the year 2006 and 2011 respectively. The break up will be 10430.20 and 11445.23 thousand tonnes for the cereals and 1076.44 and 1179.92 thousand tonnes of pulses for the two time periods. The requirement for food grains in 2006 by different age groups will be highest in adults (men) i.e. 5533.71 thousand tonnes followed by 4284.00 thousand tonnes for adults (women), 431.39 thousand tonnes for 7-9 years (children), 362.47 thousand tonnes for 4-6 years (children), 352.86 thousand tonnes for 10-12 years (boys), 293.49 thousand tonnes for 10-12 years (girls) and 248.72 thousand tonnes for 1-3 years (infants). By the year 2011, the food grains requirement will be highest in adults (men) i.e.6177.88 thousand tonnes followed by 4781.52 thousand tonnes for adults (women), 458.91thousand tonnes for 7-9 years (children), 393.05 thousand tonnes for 4-6 years (children), 285.83 thousand tonnes for 1-3 years (infants), 287.37 thousand tonnes for 10-12 years (boys) and 240.59 thousand tonnes for 10-12 years (girls).

Table 3.28: Forecasted requirement* for cereals and pulses by age groups in 2006 and 2011

(in thousand tonnes)

Food groups	*Cereals*		*Pulses*	
Year/Age groups	*2006*	*2011*	*2006*	*2011*
1-3 years	207.27 (188.43)	238.19 (216.54)	41.45 (37.68)	47.64 (43.31)

4-6 years		320.88 (291.71)	347.98 (316.34)	41.59 (37.81)	45.07 (40.97)
7-9 years		386.10 (351.00)	410.73 (373.39)	45.29 (41.17)	48.18 (43.80)
10-12 years	Boys	318.71 (289.74)	259.56 (235.96)	34.15 (31.04)	27.81 (25.28)
	Girls	262.42 (238.56)	215.12 (195.56)	31.07 (28.24)	25.47 (23.15)
Adults	Men	5048.30 (4589.36)	5635.96 (5123.60)	485.41 (441.28)	541.92 (492.65)
Women		3886.52 (3533.20)	4337.69 (3943.35)	397.48 (361.34)	443.83 (403.48)
Total		10430.20 (9482.00)	11445.23 (10404.75)	1076.44 (978.58)	1179.92 (1072.65)

*Forecasted requirement is at retail level.
Figure in parenthesis indicates the forecasted requirement at physiological level.

3.14.4 CONCLUSION

The estimates of food grains production and requirement indicated that overall cereals and pulses requirement would continue to be in surplus in both the periods. The net surplus of cereals in the state would be 1991.42 and 4519.21 thousand tonnes in 2005-06 and 2010-11. The net surplus of pulses in the state would be 1204.31 and 1439.19 thousand tonnes in the same periods. The per capita per day availability of food grains, excluding 0 years population age group, in the state in year 2005-06 will be 688.32 grams which increased to 794.28 grams in 2010-11. The estimated per capita per day availability (excluding 0 years population age group) of cereals would be 581.54 and 682.34 grams for the year 2005-06 and 2010-11 while the per capita per day availability of pulses is 106.78 and 111.94 grams for the same time periods. The estimated ranges i.e.

pessimistic range and optimistic range in which the per capita per day availability for cereals may vary is 514.98 to 648.11 grams and 612.69 to 752.00 grams for the year 2005-06 and 2010-11. The estimated limits for the pulses are 96.49 to 117.06 grams and 99.45 to 124.44 grams for the same periods.

3.15
TAMIL NADU

The state of Tamil Nadu has total geographical area of about 13,007 thousand hectares.The population of the state, as per census 2001, is 62,405,679 out of which about 44.0% of population resides in urban area. The sex ratio (i.e. females per thousand males) and population density (average number of persons per sq km) is 987 and 480 respectively. The total literacy rate in state is 73.5% which comprises 92.4% for male as against 64.4% for females. The state is bounded on north by Andhra Pradesh and Karnataka, on west by Kerala, on east by the Bay of Bengal and on south by the Indian ocean.

The economy of the state is largely depend upon agricultural sector. The major food crops are rice, jowar, ragi, bajra, maize and pulses. Important commercial crops that are grown in Tamil Nadu are sugarcane, cotton, groundnut, sesame, sunflower, castor, chillies, banana, mango, coffee, tea, rubber, cashew and coconut.

3.15.1 PROJECTIONS OF FOOD GRAINS PRODUCTION

The projections of food grains separately for the cereals and pulses for the state of Tamil Nadu at lower (pessimistic), expected (normal) and upper (optimistic) level for the year 2005-06 and 2010-11 is presented in the Table 3.29.

Table 3.29: Forecasted production of cereals and pulses for the year 2005-06 and 2010-11

(in thousand tonnes)

Crop groups	*Cereals*		*Pulses*	
Year /Production	*2005-06*	*2010-11*	*2005-06*	*2010-11*
Forecasted gross production	8955.85	9470.80	315.35	315.35

95% forecasted gross production prediction interval		8955.85 ± 430.36	9470.80± 572.39	315.35 ± 183.14	315.35 ± 120.26
Forecasted net production	Lower range level	7459.80	7786.11	115.68	170.70
	Expected range level	7836.37	8286.95	275.93	275.93
	Upper range level	8212.93	8787.79	436.18	381.16

The scrutiny of Table 3.29 reveals that the production of food grains in 2005-06 at lower range level will be 7575.48 thousand tonnes with break up of 7459.80 thousand tonnes for cereals and 115.68 thousand tonnes for the pulses. By the year 2010-11, the production will be 7956.81 thousand tonnes with the break up of 7786.11 thousand tonnes for cereals and 170.70 thousand tonnes for pulses.

At upper range level, the production of food grains in 2005-06 will be 8649.11 thousand tonnes with break up of 8212.93 thousand tonnes for cereals and 436.18 thousand tonnes for pulses. By the year 2010-11, the production will be 9168.95 thousand tonnes with the break up of 8787.79 thousand tonnes for cereals and 381.16 thousand tonnes for pulses.

The food grains production in Tamil Nadu state at the expected range level in 2005-06 will be 8112.30 thousand tonnes which will further grow to 8562.88 thousand tonnes in 2010-11. The production of cereals increased from 7836.37 thousand tonnes in 2005-06 to 8286.95 thousand tonnes in 2010-11. The production of pulses in the year 2005-06 is projected to 275.93 thousand tonnes and maintained the same level in 2010-11.

3.15.2 ESTIMATES OF POPULATION DISTRIBUTION BY AGE GROUPS

The estimated population distribution for the state of Tamil nadu by different age groups required for the projection of food grains requirement for the year 2006 and 2011 is shown in Fig. 3.29 and 3.30.

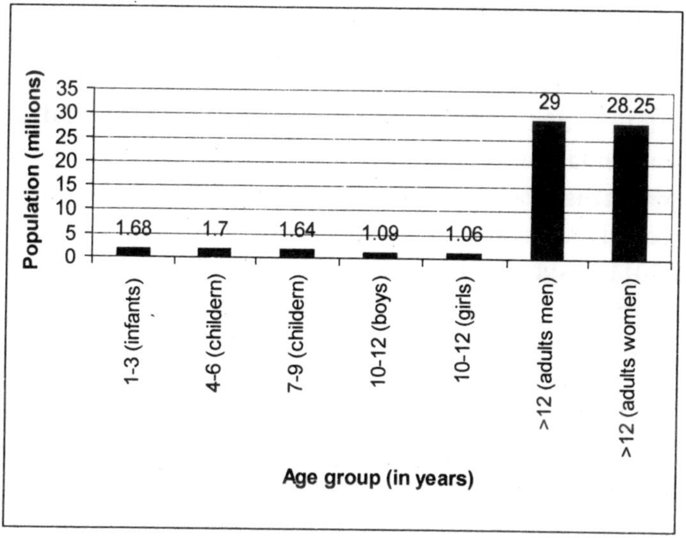

Fig. 3.29: Population distribution by age groups in 2006

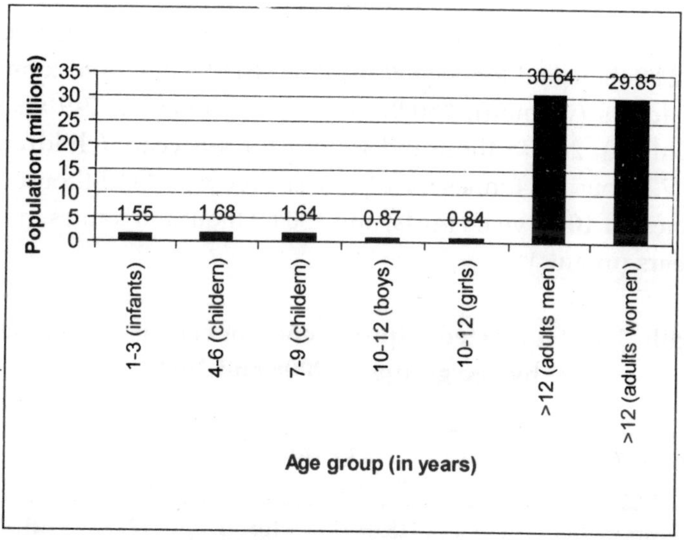

Fig. 3.30: Population distribution by age groups in 2011

3.15.3 PROJECTIONS OF FOOD GRAINS REQUIREMENT

The projections for food grain requirement by different age groups separately for cereals and pulses, on the basis of balanced diet has been estimated for the year 2006 and 2011 and the same is given in Table 3.30. On the basis of constructed population distribution by age groups and balanced diet recommendation for cereals and pulses, the estimated results show that the food grains requirement for the Tamil Nadu state will be 13122.62 and 13717.82 thousand tonnes for the year 2006 and 2011 respectively. The break up will be 11917.37 and 12460.78 thousand tonnes for the cereals and 1205.25 and 1257.04 thousand tonnes of pulses for the two time periods. The requirement for food grains in 2006 by different age groups will be highest in adults (men) i.e. 6636.09 thousand tonnes followed by 5499.69 thousand tonnes for adults (women), 250.87 thousand tonnes for 7-9 years children, 208.18 thousand tonnes for 4-6 years (children), 204.29 thousand tonnes for 10-12 years (boys), 181.85 thousand tonnes for 10-12 years (girls), and 141.65 thousand tonnes for 1-3 years (infants). By the year 2011, the food grains requirement will be highest in adults (men) i.e. 7012.88 thousand tonnes followed by 5811.95 thousand tonnes for adults (women), 250.87 thousand tonnes for 7-9 years (children), 205.73 thousand tonnes for 4-6 years (children), 161.72 thousand tonnes for 10-12 years (boys), 143.97 thousand tonnes for 10-12 years (girls) and 130.69 thousand tonnes for 1-3 years (infants).

Table 3.30. Forecasted requirement* for cereals and pulses by age groups in 2006 and 2011

(in thousand tonnes)

Crop groups	*Cereals*		*Pulses*	
Year /Age groups	*2005-06*	*2010-11*	*2005-06*	*2010-11*
1-3 years	118.04 (107.31)	108.91 (99.00)	23.61 (21.46)	21.78 (19.80)

4-6 years		184.29 (167.53)	182.12 (165.56)	23.89 (21.72)	23.61 (21.46)
7-9 years		224.53 (204.12)	224.53 (204.12)	26.34 (23.94)	26.34 (23.94)
10-12 years	Boys	184.52 (167.74)	146.07 (132.79)	19.77 (17.97)	15.65 (14.22)
	Girls	162.60 (147.82)	128.73 (117.02)	19.25 (17.50)	15.24 (13.85)
Adults	Men	6053.98 (5503.62)	6397.72 (5816.11)	582.11 (529.19)	615.16 (559.24)
	Women	4989.41 (4535.83)	5272.70 (4793.36)	510.28 (463.89)	539.25 (490.22)
Total		11917.37 (10833.97)	12460.78 (11327.98)	1205.25 (1095.68)	1257.04 (1142.76)

*Forecasted requirement is at retail level.
Figure in parenthesis indicates the forecasted requirement at physiological level.

3.15.4 CONCLUSION

The estimates of food grains production and requirement indicated that overall cereals and pulses requirement would continue to be in deficit condition in both the periods. The net deficit of cereals in the state would be 4081.00 and 4173.83 thousand tonnes in 2005-06 and 2010-11. The net deficit of pulses in the state would be 929.32 and 999.11 thousand tonnes in the same periods. The per capita per day availability of food grains, excluding 0 years population age group, in the state in year 2005-06 will be 345.00 grams which increased to 349.78 grams in 2010-11. The estimated per capita per day availability (excluding 0 years population age group) of cereals would be 333.27 and 338.51 grams for the year 2005-06 and 2010-11 while the per capita per day availability of pulses is 11.73 and 11.27 grams for the same time periods. The estimated ranges i.e.

pessimistic range and optimistic range in which the per capita per day availability for cereals may vary is 317.26 to 349.29 grams and 318.05 to 358.97 grams for the year 2005-06 and 2010-11. The estimated limits for the pulses are 4.92 to 18.55 grams and 6.97 to 15.57 grams for the same periods.

3.16
UTTAR PRADESH

(The analysis in this section is pertaining to Undivided Uttar Pradesh)

The Uttar Pradesh is one of the major states of the Indian Union. The new state of Uttarakhand was carved out of as 27th state of India in November, 2000. Now, after the formation of Uttarakhand, the Uttar Pradesh has total geographical area of about 2,38,56 thousand hectares. The population of the state, as per census 2001, is 166,197,921 out of which about 20.8% of population resides in urban area. The sex ratio (i.e. females per thousand males) and population density (average number of persons per sq km) is 898 and 690 respectively. The total literacy rate in state is 56.3% which comprise 68.8% for male as against 42.2% for females. The state of Uttar Pradesh is located in north India. It is bounded north-west by Himachal Pradesh, north by Tibet and Nepal, east by Bihar, south and south west by Madhya Pradesh and west by Rajasthan, Haryana and Delhi. Uttar Pradesh ranks 1st in the production of food grains, sugarcane and potato. The state ranks second in production of mustard and rapeseed and total pulses. The other crops grown in the state are cotton, oilseeds, jute, opium and sesamum,

The newly formed Uttarakhand state has total geographical area of about 5,348 thousand hectares with population of the state, as per census 2001, is 8,489,349 out of which about 25.7% of population resides in urban area. The sex ratio (i.e. females per thousand males) and population density (average number of persons per sq km) is 962 and 159 respectively. The total literacy rate in state is 71.6 which comprise 83.3% for male as against 59.6% for females.

3.16.1 PROJECTIONS OF FOOD GRAINS PRODUCTION

The projections of food grains separately for the cereals and pulses for the state of Uttar Pradesh at lower (pessimistic), expected (normal) and upper (optimistic) level for the year 2005-06 and 2010-11 is presented in the Table 3.31.

Table 3.31: Forecasted production of cereals and pulses for the year 2005-06 and 2010-11

(in thousand tonnes)

Crop groups		*Cereals*		*Pulses*	
Year /Production		*2005-06*	*2010-11*	*2005-06*	*2010-11*
Forecasted gross production		46132.26	50755.91	2147.57	2015.77
95% forecasted gross production prediction interval		46132.26± 744.01	50755.91± 989.55	2147.57± 78.17	2015.77± 103.99
Forecasted net production	Lower range level	39714.72	43545.56	1810.72	1672.81
	Expected range level	40365.73	44411.42	1879.12	1763.80
	Upper range level	41016.74	45277.28	1947.52	1854.79

The scrutiny of Table 3.31 reveals that the production of food grains in 2005-06 at lower range level will be 41525.44 thousand tonnes with break up of 39714.72 thousand tonnes for cereals and 1810.72 thousand tonnes for the pulses. By the year 2010-11, the production will be 45218.37 thousand tonnes with the break up of 43545.56 thousand tonnes for cereals and 1672.81 thousand tonnes for pulses.

At upper range level, the production of food grains in 2005-06 will be 42964.26 thousand tonnes with break up of 41016.7 thousand tonnes for cereals and 1947.52 thousand tonnes fc pulses. By the year 2010-11, the production will be 47132.0

thousand tonnes with the break up 45277.28 thousand tonnes for cereals and 1854.79 thousand tonnes for pulses.

The forecast of the food grains production in Uttar Pradesh at the expected range level in 2005-06 will be 42244.85 thousand tonnes which will further grow to 46175.22 thousand tonnes in 2010-11. There will be a growth in the production of cereals from 40365.73 thousand tonnes in 2005-06 to 44411.42 thousand tonnes in 2010-11. The production of pulses in 2005-06 is 1879.12 thousand tonnes which decreased to 1763.80 thousand tonnes in 2010-11.

3.16.2 ESTIMATES OF POPULATION DISTRIBUTION BY AGE GROUPS

The estimated population distribution for the state of Uttar Pradesh by different age groups required for the projection of food grains requirement for the year 2006 and 2011is shown in Fig. 3.31 and 3.32.

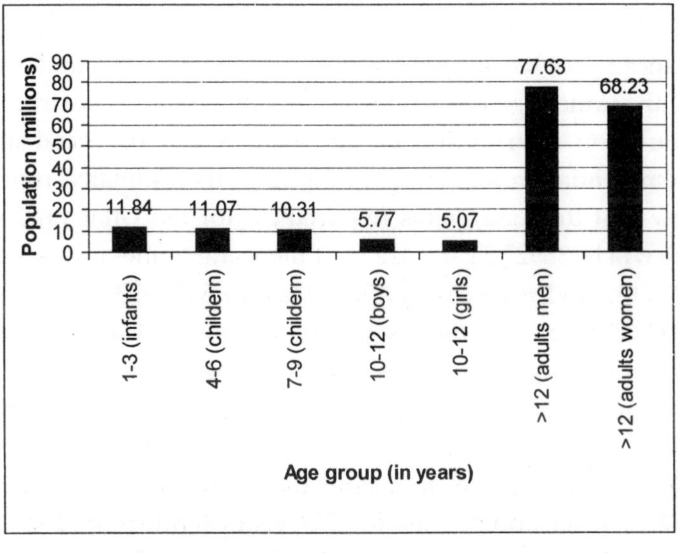

Fig. 3.31: Population distribution by age groups in 2006

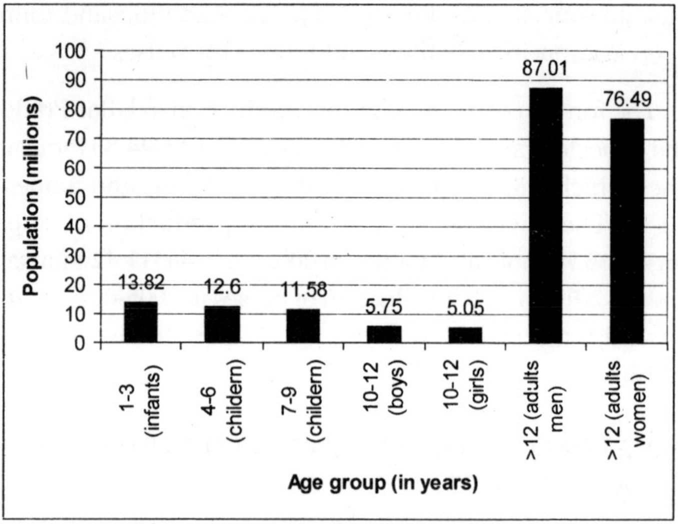

Fig. 3.32: Population distribution by age groups in 2011

3.16.3 PROJECTIONS OF FOOD GRAINS REQUIREMENT

The projections for food grain requirement by different age groups separately for cereals and pulses, on the basis of balanced diet has been estimated for the year 2006 and 2011 and the same is given in Table 3.32. On the basis of constructed population distribution by age groups and balanced diet recommendation for cereals and pulses, the estimated results show that the food grains requirement for the Uttar Pradesh state will be 36925.54 and 41222.31 thousand tonnes for the year 2006 and 2011 respectively. The break up will be 33451.01 and 37341.23 thousand tonnes for the cereals and 3474.53 and 3881.08 thousand tonnes of pulses for the two time periods. The requirement for food grains in 2006 by different age groups will be highest in adults (men) i.e. 17765.19 thousand tonnes followed by 13286.96 thousand tonnes for adults (women) 1577.14 thousand tonnes for 7-9 years (children), 1355.60 thousand tonnes for 4-6 years (children), 1077.06 thousand tonnes for 10-12 years (boys), 998.29 thousand tonnes for 1-3 years (infants) and 865.30 thousand tonnes for 10-12 years (girls). By the year 2011, the food grains requirement will be highest in adults (men) i.e. 19913.67 thousand tonnes followed by 14893.85 thousand tonnes for adults (women), 1771.40 thousand tonnes for 7-9 years (children), 1542.96 thousand tonnes for 4-6 years (children), 1073.09 thousand tonnes for 10-12 years (boys), 1165.24thousand tonnes for 1-3 years (infants) and 862.10 thousand tonnes for 10-12 years (girls).

Table 3.32. Forecasted requirement* for cereals and pulses by age groups in 2006 and 2011

(in thousand tonnes)

Food groups		*Cereals*		*Pulses*	
Year /Age groups		*2005-06*	*2010-11*	*2005-06*	*2010-11*
1-3 years		831.91 (756.28)	971.03 (882.75)	166.38 (151.25)	194.21 (176.55)
4-6 years		1200.04 (1090.94)	1365.90 (1241.73)	155.56 (141.42)	177.06 (160.96)
7-9 years		1411.56 (1283.23)	1585.43 (1441.30)	165.58 (150.53)	185.97 (169.06)
10-12 years	Boys	972.83 (884.39)	969.24 (881.13)	104.23 (94.75)	103.85 (94.41)
	Girls	773.68 (703.34)	770.82 (700.74)	91.62 (83.29)	91.28 (82.98)
Adults	Men	16206.84 (14733.49)	18166.86 (16515.33)	1558.35 (1416.68)	1746.81 (1588.00)
	Women	12054.15 (10958.32)	13511.95 (12283.59)	1232.81 (1120.74)	1381.90 (1256.27)
Total		33451.01 (30410.00)	37341.23 (33946.57)	3474.53 (3158.66)	3881.08 (3528.25)

*Forecasted requirement is at retail level.

Figure in parenthesis indicates the forecasted requirement at physiological level.

3.16.4 CONCLUSION

The estimates of food grains production and requirement indicated that the cereals requirement would continue to be in surplus condition while pulses requirement would continue to be in deficit condition in both the periods. The surplus of cereals in the state would be 6914.72 and 7070.19 thousand tonnes in 2005-06 and 2010-11. The deficit of pulses in the state would be 1595.41 and 2117.28 thousand tonnes in the same periods. The per capita per day availability of food grains, excluding 0 years population age group, in the state in year 2005-06 will be 607.41 grams which decreased to 595.89 grams in 2010-11. The estimated per capita per day availability (excluding 0 years population age group) of cereals would be 580.30 and 573.13 grams for the year 2005-06 and 2010-11 while the per capita per day availability of pulses is 27.11 and 22.76 grams for the same time periods. The estimated ranges i.e. pessimistic range and optimistic range in which the per capita per day availability for cereals may vary is 572.91 to 591.69 grams and 561.95 to 584.30 grams for the year 2005-06 and 2010-11. The estimated limits for the pulses is 26.12 to 28.09 grams and 21.59 to 23.94 grams for the same periods.

3.17
WEST BENGAL

The state of West Bengal has total geographical area of about 8,775 thousand hectares. The population of the state, as per census 2001, is 80,176,197 out of which about 28% of population resides in urban area. The sex ratio (i.e. females per thousand males) and population density (average number of persons per sq km) is 934 and 903 respectively. The total literacy rate in state is 68.6% which comprises 77.0% for male as against 59.6% for females. The land frontiers of the state touches Bangladesh in the east and is separated from Nepal in the west. Bhutan lies in the north east while Sikkim is on the north. On the west and south are the states of Bihar, Jharkhand and Orissa, respectively.

The agriculture sector in West Bengal is characterized by the predominance of small and marginal farmers having more than 68% of the total operated area of the state. The average size of holding here is less than one hectare. The state ranks first in production of rice in the country and also remarkable progress has been made during the last one decade in the production of oilseeds. West Bengal also produces more than 60% of the country's raw jute fiber.

3.17.1 PROJECTIONS OF FOOD GRAINS PRODUCTION

The projections of food grains separately for the cereals and pulses for the state of West Bengal at lower (pessimistic), expected (normal) and upper (optimistic) level for the year 2005-06 and 2010-11 is presented in the Table 3.33.

Table 3.33: Forecasted production of cereals and pulses for the year 2005-06 and 2010-11

(in thousand tonnes)

Crop groups		*Cereals*		*Pulses*	
Year /Production		*2005-06*	*2010-11*	*2005-06*	*2010-11*
Forecasted gross production		14975.77	14742.84	102.22	83.53
95% forecasted gross production prediction interval		14975.77± 237.90	14742.84± 400.42	102.22 ± 34.26	83.53 ± 32.98
Forecasted net production	Lower range level	12895.64	12549.62	59.46	44.23
	Expected range level	13103.80	12899.98	89.44	73.09
	Upper range level	13311.96	13250.35	119.42	101.95

The scrutiny of Table 3.33 reveals that the production of food grains in 2005-06 at lower range level will be 12955.10 thousand tonnes with break up of 12895.64 thousand tonnes for cereals and 59.46 thousand tonnes for the pulses. By the year 2010-11, the production will be 12593.85 thousand tonnes with the break up of 12549.62 thousand tonnes for cereals and 44.23 thousand tonnes for pulses.

At upper range level, the production of food grains in 2005-06 will be 13431.38 thousand tonnes with break up of 13311.96thousand tonnes for cereals and 119.42 thousand tonnes for pulses. By the year 2010-11, the production will be 13352.30 thousand tonnes with the break up 13250.35 thousand tonnes for cereals and 101.95 thousand tonnes for pulses.

The forecast of the production of food grains production in West Bengal at the expected range level in 2005-06 will be 13193.24 thousand tonnes which decreased to 12973.07 thousand tonnes in 2010-11. The production of cereals is decreased from 13103.80 thousand tonnes in 2005-06 to 12899.98 thousand tonnes in 2010-11.The production of pulses in 2005-06 is 89.44 thousand tonnes which decreased to 73.09 thousand tonnes in 2010-11.

3.17.2 ESTIMATES OF POPULATION DISTRIBUTION BY AGE GROUPS

The estimated population distribution for the state of West Bengal by different age groups required for the projection of food grains requirement for the year 2006 and 2011 is shown in Fig. 3.33 and 3.34.

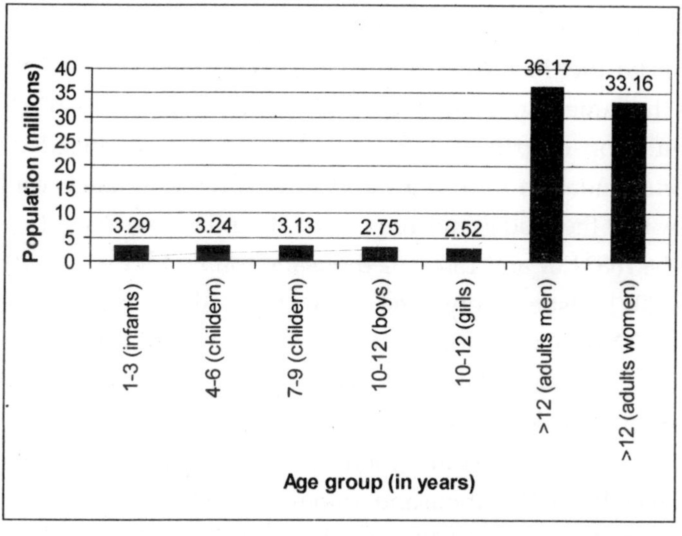

Fig. 3.33: Population distribution by age groups in 2006

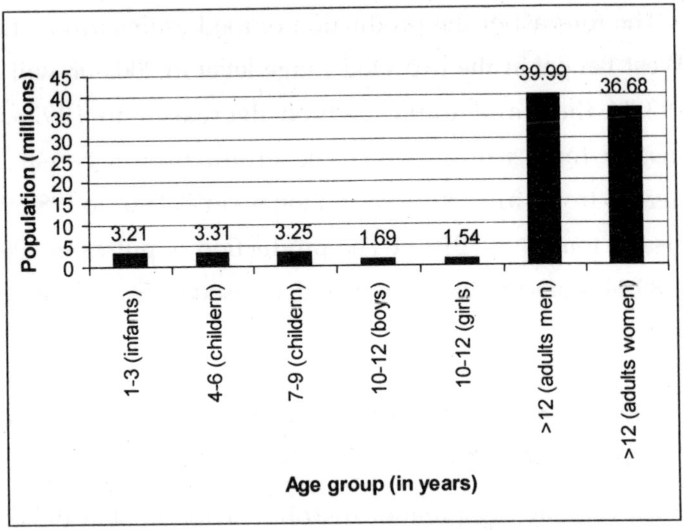

Fig. 3.34: Population distribution by age groups in 2011

3.17.3 PROJECTIONS OF FOOD GRAINS REQUIREMENT

The projections for food grain requirement by different age groups separately for cereals and pulses, on the basis of balanced diet has been estimated for the year 2006 and 2011 and the same is given in Table 3.34. On the basis of constructed population distribution by age groups and balanced diet recommendation for cereals and pulses, the estimated results show that the food grains requirement for the west Bengal state will be 16831.07 and 18046.02 thousand tonnes for the year 2006 and 2011 respectively. The break up will be 15268.60 and 16378.32 thousand tonnes for the cereals and 1562.47 and 1667.70 thousand tonnes of pulses for the two time periods. The requirement for food grains in 2006 by different age groups will be highest in adults (men) i.e. 8276.74 thousand tonnes followed by 6457.97 thousand tonnes for adults (women), 513.26 thousand tonnes for 10-12 years (boys), 478.80 thousand tonnes for 7-9 years (children), 430.15 thousand tonnes for 10-12 years (girls), 396.76 thousand tonnes for 4-6 years (children) and 277.39 thousand tonnes for 1-3 years (infants). By the year 2011, the food grains requirement will be highest in adults (men) i.e. 9153.00 thousand tonnes followed by 7141.67 thousand tonnes for adults (women), 497.15 thousand tonnes for 7-9 years (children), 405.33 thousand tonnes for 4-6 years (children), 314.56 thousand tonnes for 10-12 years (boys), 270.65 thousand tonnes for 1-3 years (infants) and 263.65 thousand tonnes for 10-12 years (girls).

Table 3.34. Forecasted requirement* for cereals and pulses by age groups in 2006 and 2011

(in thousand tonnes)

Crop groups		*Cereals*		*Pulses*	
Year/Age groups		*2006*	*2011*	*2006*	*2011*
1-3 years		231.16 (210.14)	225.54 (205.04)	46.23 (42.03)	45.11 (41.00)
4-6 years		351.23 (319.30)	358.82 (326.20)	45.53 (41.39)	46.51 (42.28)
7-9 years		428.53 (389.57)	444.96 (404.51)	50.27 (45.70)	52.19 (47.44)
10-12 years	Boys	463.59 (421.44)	284.12 (258.29)	49.67 (45.15)	30.44 (27.67)
	Girls	384.61 (349.64)	235.73 (214.30)	45.54 (41.40)	27.92 (25.38)
Adults	Men	7550.71 (6864.28)	8350.11 (7591.00)	726.03 (660.03)	802.89 (729.90)
	Women	5858.77 (5326.15)	6479.04 (5890.04)	599.20 (544.73)	662.63 (602.39)
Total		15268.60 (13880.54)	16378.32 (14889.38)	1562.47 (1420.42)	1667.70 (1516.09)

*Forecasted requirement is at retail level.

Figure in parenthesis indicates the forecasted requirement at physiological level.

3.17.4 CONCLUSION

The estimates of food grains production and requirement indicated that overall cereals and pulses requirement would continue to be in deficit in both the periods. The deficit of cereals in the state would be 2164.8 and 3478.34 thousand tonnes in 2005-06 and 2010-11. The deficit of pulses in the state would be 1473.03 and 1594.61 thousand tonnes in the same periods. The per capita per day availability of food grains, excluding 0 years population age group, in the state in year 2005-06 will be 426.07 grams which decreased to 396.37 grams in 2010-11. The estimated per capita per day availability (excluding 0 years population age group) of cereals would be 426.07 and 394.14 grams for the year 2005-06 and 2010-11 while the per capita per day availability of pulses is 2.91 and 2.23 grams for the same time periods. The estimated ranges i.e. pessimistic range and optimistic range in which the per capita per day availability for cereals may vary is 419.30 to 432.84 grams and 383.83 to 404.84 grams for the year 2005-06 and 2010-11. The estimated limits for the pulses are 1.93 to 3.88 grams and 1.35 to 3.11 grams for the same periods.

CHAPTER 4

NATIONAL FOOD GRAINS SUPPLY AND REQUIREMENT-SYNTHESIS OF MAJOR STATES

As already given, the major states selected in the present study accounts approximately 97% of total population (1991) and food grains production (1998-99) in India. The purpose of the present chapter is to synthesize the result of analysis of 17 major states approximated at national level. The selected states in the study are Andhra Pradesh, Assam, Bihar, Gujarat, Haryana, Himachal Pradesh, Jammu and Kashmir Karnataka, Kerala, Madhya Pradesh, Maharashtra, Orissa, Punjab, Rajasthan, Tamil Nadu, Uttar Pradesh and West Bengal.

The present chapter consist of six sections. The section I i.e. 4.1 concludes the projections of food grains production at lower, expected and upper range level of the major states. The section 4.2 deals to determine the estimates of population distribution by age groups of the major states. The section 4.3 aggregates the food grains requirement of all major states. The per capita per day availability of food grains at lower, expected and upper range level is given in section 4.4. The section 4.5 is devoted to analyze the food grains production-requirement gap. Section 4.6 attempts to cover the estimation of foodgrains storage requirement at the national level for the year 2005-06 and 2010-11. The purpose of the comparative analysis of major states *via* section 4.4 and 4.5 is to frame some important policy implications. The main purpose is to see that which state would continue to be backbone of nation's food security.

4.1 FORECAST OF THE FOOD GRAINS PRODUCTION AT LOWER, EXPECTED AND UPPER RANGE LEVEL OF THE MAJOR STATES

The forecast production of food grains in 2005-06 and 2010-11 at lower range level for all the major states is given in Fig. 4.1. It is shown in figure that the production of food grains in 2005-06 will be 189.44 million tonnes with break up of 177.10 million tonnes for cereals and 12.34 million tonnes for the pulses. By the year 2010-11, the production will be 205.76 million tonnes with the break up of 192.83 million tonnes for cereals and 12.93 million tonnes for pulses.

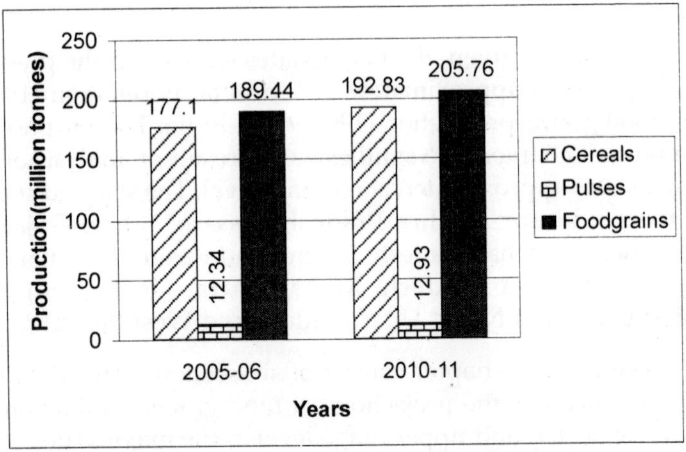

Fig. 4.1: Food grains production at lower range level in 2005-06 and 2010-11

The forecast of the food grains production in all the major states at the expected range level is given in Fig. 4.2. The production of food grain in 2005-06 is projected to 201.10 million tonnes with a break up of 187.39 and 13.71 million tonnes. The food grains production in 2010-11 will grow upto 220.21 million tonnes with a break up of 205.65 and 14.56 million tonnes.

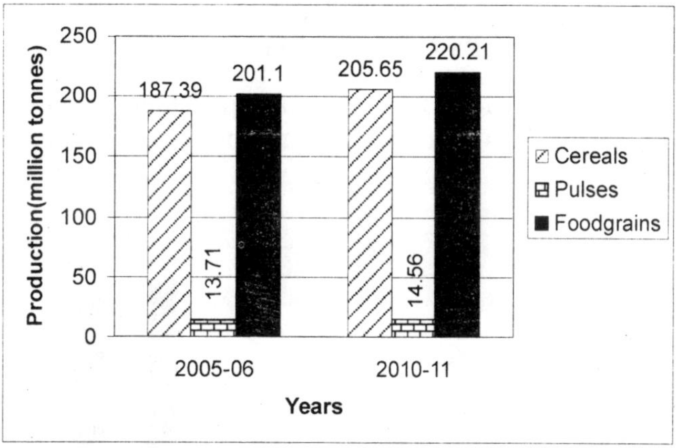

Fig. 4.2: Food grains production at expected range level in 2005-06 and 2010-11

At upper range level (Fig. 4.3), the forecasting results shows that the production of food grains in 2005-06 will be 212.76 thousand tonnes with break up of 197.69 million tonnes for cereals and 15.07 thousand tonnes for pulses. By the year 2010-11, the production will be 234.69 million tonnes with the break up of 218.48 million tonnes for cereals and 16.21 million tonnes for pulses.

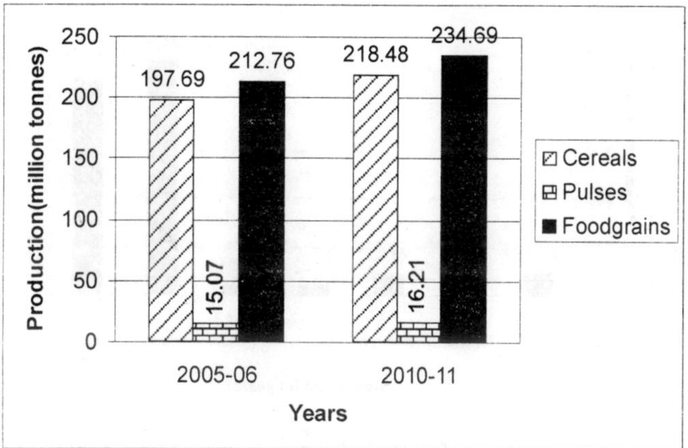

Fig. 4.3: Food grains production at upper range level in 2005-06 and 2010-11

4.2 ESTIMATES OF POPULATION DISTRIBUTION BY AGE GROUPS OF THE MAJOR STATES

The estimation of food grains requirement requires the corresponding population figures (except the age group of zero

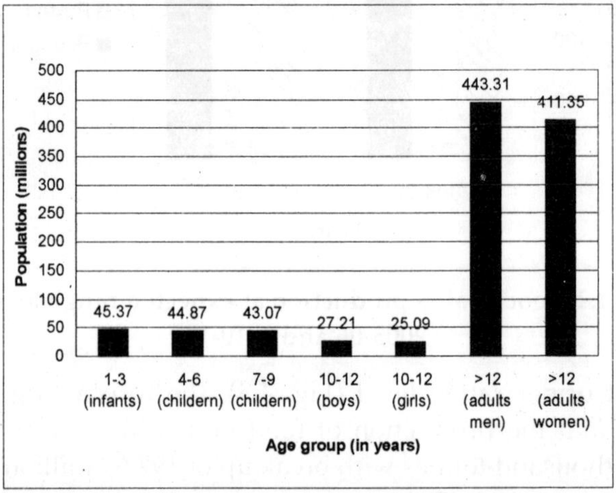

Fig. 4.4: Population distribution by age groups of the major states in 2006

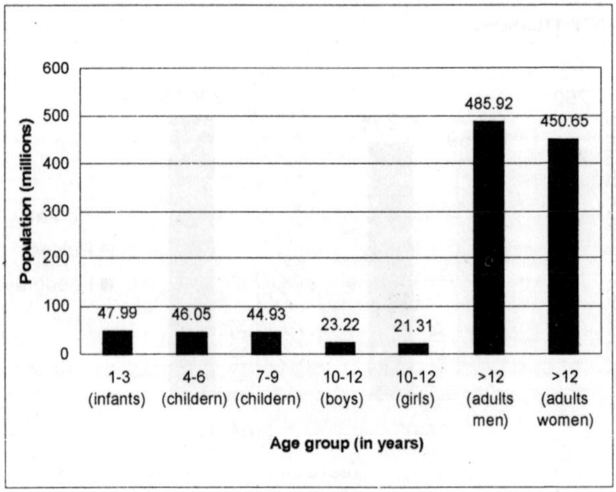

Fig. 4.5: Population distribution by age groups of the major states in 2011

year) for the different age groups, which were estimated as on 1st March, for the year 2006 and 2011. The estimated population distribution for all the major states by different age groups required for the projection of food grains requirement for the two time periods is shown in Fig. 4.4 and 4.5.

4.3 FOOD GRAINS REQUIREMENT OF THE MAJOR STATES

The projections for food grain requirement by different age groups separately for cereals and pulses for the major states has been estimated for the year 2006 and 2011 and the same is shown in Figs. 4.6, 4.7 and 4.8. On the basis of constructed population distribution by age groups and balanced diet recommendation for cereals and pulses, the estimated results show that the food grains requirement for all the major states by different age groups will be 206.81 and 223.46 million tonnes for the year 2006 and 2011 respectively. The break up will be 187.58 and 202.73 million tonnes for the cereals and 19.23 and 20.73 million tonnes of pulses for the two time periods. The requirement for food grains in 2006 by different age groups will be highest in adults (men) i.e. 101.45 million tonnes followed by 80.1 million tonnes for adults (women), 6.58 million tonnes for 7-9 years (children), 5.49 million tonnes for 4-6 years (children), 5.08 million tonnes for 10-12 years (boys), 4.28 million tonnes for 10-12 years (girls) and 3.83 million tonnes for 1-3 years (infants). By the year 2011, the food grains requirement will be highest in adults (men) i.e. 111.20 million tonnes followed by 87.75 million tonnes for adults (women), 6.87 million tonnes for 7-9 years (children), 5.64 million tonnes for 4-6 years (children), 4.33 million tonnes for 10-12 years (boys), 4.04 million tonnes for 1-3 years (infants) and 3.63 million tonnes for 10-12 years (girls).

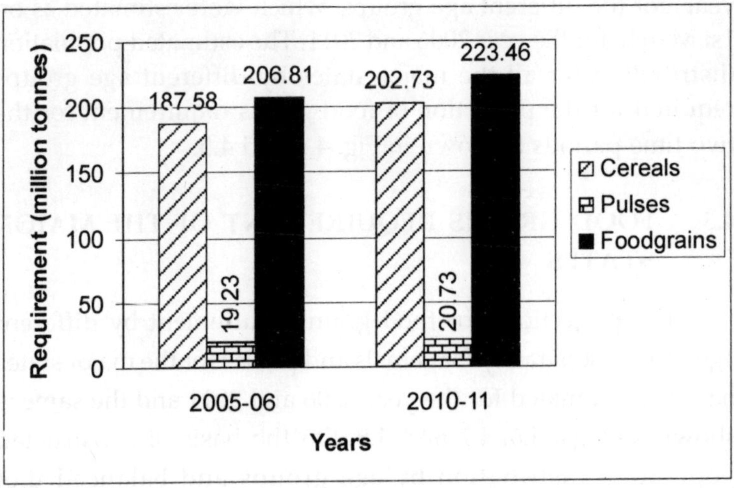

Fig. 4.6: Food grains requirement of the major states in the year 2006 and 2011.

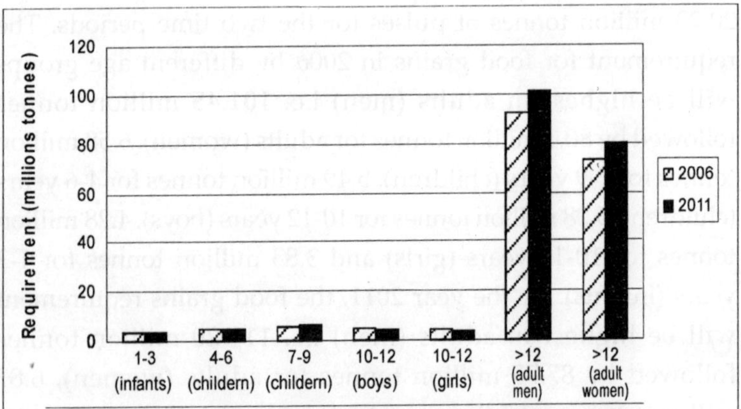

	1-3 (infants)	4-6 (childern)	7-9 (childern)	10-12 (boys)	10-12 (girls)	>12 (adult men)	>12 (adult women)
2006	3.19	4.86	5.89	4.59	3.83	92.55	72.67
2011	3.37	4.99	6.15	3.91	3.25	101.45	79.61

Age group (in years)

Fig. 4.7: Cereals requirement by age groups of the major states in 2006 and 2011.

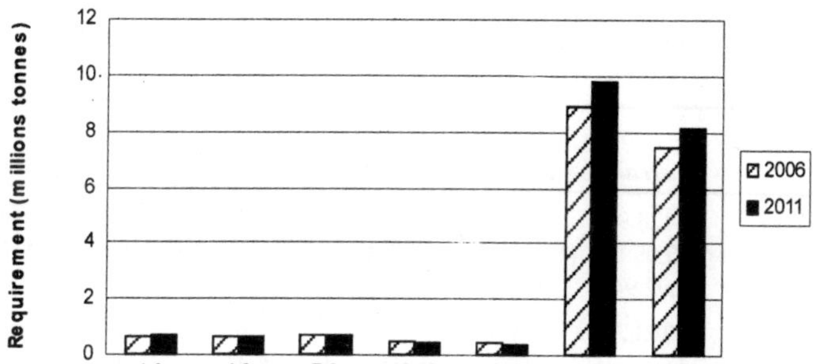

	1-3 (infants)	4-6 (childern)	7-9 (childern)	10-12 (boys)	10-12 (girls)	>12 (adult men)	>12 (adult women)
2006	0.64	0.63	0.69	0.49	0.45	8.9	7.43
2011	0.67	0.65	0.72	0.42	0.38	9.75	8.14

Age group (in years)

Fig. 4.8: Pulses requirement by age groups of the major states in 2006 and 2011.

4.4 PER CAPITA PER DAY AVAILABILITY OF FOOD GRAINS AT LOWER, EXPECTED AND UPPER RANGE LEVEL

The expected per capita per day availability of food grains for the major states, in the year 2005-06 and 2010-11 is shown in Table 4.1. In the year 2005-06, the expected per capita per day availability of food grains is highest for the state of Punjab, followed by the state of Haryana, Rajasthan, Madhya Pradesh, Uttar Pradesh, Himachal Pradesh, Karnataka, Andhra Pradesh, West Bengal, Orissa, Maharashtra, Assam, Jammu and Kashmir, Tamil Nadu, Bihar, Gujarat and Kerala. By the year 2010-11, the expected per capita per day availability of food grains is highest for the state of Punjab, followed by the state of Haryana, Rajasthan, Madhya Pradesh, Uttar Pradesh, Himachal Pradesh, Karnataka, Andhra Pradesh, Orrisa, West Bengal, Maharashtra, Assam, Tamil Nadu, Jammu and Kashmir, Bihar, Gujarat and Kerala.

Table 4.1: Expected per capita per day availability of food grains, major states, in the year 2005-06 and 2010-11

(in grams)

S. No	States	2005-06 Cereals	2005-06 Pulses	2005-06 Food grains	2010-11 Cereals	2010-11 Pulses	2010-11 Food grains
1.	Andhra Pradesh	428.99 (365.05 to 492.94)	24.48 (19.04 to 29.93)	453.48 (384.09 to 522.87)	449.45 (368.61 to 530.29)	24.96 (18.29 to 31.62)	474.41 (386.90 to 561.91)
2.	Assam	353.79 (344.46 to 363.12)	6.58 (5.47 to 7.70)	360.38 (349.93 to 370.82)	357.62 (346.05 to 369.18)	6.97 (4.08 to 9.86)	364.59 (350.13 to 379.04)
3.	Bihar	323.90 (310.88 to 336.92)	12.83 (9.95 to 15.74)	336.74 (320.83 to 352.66)	323.05 (307.19 to 338.91)	10.40 (6.29 to 14.50)	333.45 (313.48 to 353.41)
4.	Gujarat	259.56 (234.68 to 284.48)	35.99 (32.77 to 39.20)	295.55 (267.45 to 323.68)	269.22 (238.21 to 300.22)	38.02 (36.17 to 39.88)	307.24 (274.38 to 340.10)
5.	Haryana	1590.19 (1398.90 to 1781.47)	44.42 (28.41 to 60.42)	1634.61 (1427.31 to 1841.49)	1668.88 (1471.20 to 1866.55)	41.20 (26.96 to 53.06)	1710.08 (1498.16 to 1919.61)
6.	Himachal	502.47 (437.07 to 567.88)	4.86 (4.45 to 5.27)	507.33 (441.52 to 573.15)	498.86 (439.34 to 558.39)	5.02 (4.51 to 5.53)	503.88 (443.85 to 563.92)
7.	Jammu & Kashmir	345.67 (333.88 to 357.46)	2.18 (1.82 to 2.53)	347.85 (335.70 to 359.99)	347.67 (332.78 to 362.56)	1.18 (0.73 to 1.74)	348.85 (333.51 to 364.30)
8.	Karnataka	435.42 (421.24 to 449.42)	35.55 (33.79 to 37.31)	470.97 (455.03 to 486.73)	452.52 (434.87 to 470.17)	37.29 (35.08 to 39.49)	489.81 (469.95 to 509.66)
9.	Kerala	48.84 (38.13 to 59.54)	1.5 (0.75 to 2.26)	50.34 (38.88 to 61.80)	39.95 (25.43 to 54.47)	1.45 (0.38 to 2.52)	41.40 (25.81 to 56.99)
10.	Madhya Pradesh	511.31 (496.31 to 526.30)	114.76 (111.79 to 117.74)	626.07 (608.10 to 644.04)	511.99 (493.71 to 530.27)	111.40 (107.78 to 115.02)	623.39 (601.49 to 645.29)
11.	Maharashtra	310.08 (288.13 to 332.03)	61.31 (56.90 to 65.72)	371.39 (345.03 to 397.75)	316.74 (289.07 to 344.41)	65.56 (59.21 to 71.92)	382.30 (348.28 to 416.33)
12.	Orissa	403.28 (334.27 to 472.28)	20.72 (12.88 to 28.57)	424.00 (347.15 to 500.85)	395.69 (329.21 to 462.17)	19.78 (12.29 to 27.27)	415.47 (341.50 to 489.44)

13. Punjab	2476.77 (2436.33 to 2517.21)	2.74 (1.25 to 4.22)	2479.51 (2437.58 to 2521.43)	2556.04 (2505.14 to 2606.93)	1.71 (0.24 to 3.18)	2557.75 (2505.38 to 2610.11)
14. Rajasthan	581.54 (514.98 to 648.11)	106.78 (96.49 to 117.06)	688.32 (611.47 to 765.17)	682.34 (612.69 to 752.00)	111.94 (99.45 to 124.44)	794.28 (712.14 to 876.44)
15. Tamil Nadu	333.27 (317.26 to 349.29)	11.73 (4.92 to 18.55)	345.00 (322.18 to 367.84)	338.51 (318.05 to 358.97)	11.27 (6.97 to 15.57)	349.78 (325.02 to 374.54)
16. Uttar Pradesh	580.30 (572.91 to 591.69)	27.11 (26.12 to 28.09)	607.41 (599.03 to 619.78)	573.13 (561.95 to 584.30)	22.76 (21.59 to 23.94)	595.89 (583.54 to 608.24)
17. West Bengal	426.07 (419.30 to 432.84)	2.91 (1.93 to 3.88)	428.98 (421.23 to 436.72)	394.14 (383.83 to 404.84)	2.23 (1.35 to 3.11)	396.37 (385.18 to 407.95)
Average	493.53 (466.42 to 520.64)	36.11 (32.51 to 39.71)	529.64 (498.93 to 560.35)	503.04 (471.67 to 534.42)	35.63 (31.63 to 39.58)	538.67 (503.30 to 574.00)

Figures in parenthesis are the pessimistic and optimistic ranges in which per capita per day availability of food grains may vary.

4.5 FOOD GRAINS PRODUCTION REQUIREMENT GAP

The estimated food grains production requirement gap for the major states for the year is 2005-06 and 2010-11 given in Table 4.2. While looking at the production requirement balances for food grains, it seems that the cereal and pulses will be in deficit condition in the year 2005-06.The requirement of cereals would be met with marginal surplus in the year 2010-11 while the requirement of pulses would remain in deficit condition, in both the periods.

Looking at the comparative features of different states for the year 2005-06, the largest surplus of cereals will be contributed by Punjab followed by Haryana, Uttar Pradesh, Rajasthan, Madhya Pradesh and with a marginal surplus by the state of Himachal Pradesh. In case of pulses, the largest surplus would be contributed by Madhya Pradesh followed by Rajasthan and Maharashtra. The results shows that the only Madhya Pradesh and Rajasthan would be the states which can fulfill the requirement of cereals and pulses both but the largest contribution of food grains to the nation will be provided by the Punjab followed by Haryana, Uttar Pradesh, Rajasthan and Madhya Pradesh because of the surplus of cereals. By the year 2010-11, the same pattern follows.

Table 4.2: Estimated food grains production-requirement gap in 2005-06 and 2010-11

(in thousand tonnes)

S.No.	*States*	*Production requirement gap (2005-06)*		*Production requirement gap (2010-11)*	
		Cereals	*Pulses*	*Cereals*	*Pulses*
1.	Andhra Pradesh	(-)2119.20	(-)772.81	(-)1684.97	(-)801.82
2.	Assam	(-)1458.47	(-)451.87	(-)1534.44	(-)481.09
3.	Bihar	(-)6640.69	(-)1499.10	(-)7163.64	(-)1738.63
4.	Gujrat	(-)4463.61	(-)278.85	(-)4639.16	(-)259.58
5.	Haryana	(+)8552.16	(-)48.54	(+)9857.62	(-)80.47
6.	Himachal Pradesh	(+)59.05	(-)120.74	(+)12.44	(-)129.96
7.	Jammu & Kashmir	(-)534.89	(-)190.08	(-)627.75	(-)207.89
8.	Karnataka	(-)1272.29	(-)309.77	(-)1034.55	(-)293.64
9.	Kerala	(-)5618.50	(-)612.39	(-)5993.41	(-)639.14
10.	Madhya Pradesh	(+)719.21	(+)2044.25	(+)545.89	(+)2101.01
11.	Maharashtra	(-)6711.41	(+)361.93	(-)6939.97	(+)534.77
12.	Orissa	(-)1396.01	(-)416.43	(-)1596.65	(-)450.93
13.	Punjab	(+)18025.22	(-)439.67	(+)19772.21	(-)476.27
14.	Rajasthan	(+)1991.42	(+)1204.31	(+)4519.21	(+)1439.19
15.	Tamil Nadu	(-)4081.00	(-)929.32	(-)4173.83	(-)981.11
16.	Uttar Pradesh	(+)6914.72	(-)1595.41	(+)7070.19	(-)2117.28
17.	West Bengal	(-)2164.80	(-)1473.03	(-)3478.34	(-)1594.61
Average		(-)199.09	(-)5527.52	(+)2910.85	(-)6177.45

Note: (+) indicates surplus while (-) indicates deficit.

As the major states selected in the present study accounts about 97% of total population (1991) and food grains production (1998-99) in India. Keeping this in view and assuming that on an average same production pattern and growth of population will also follow in other parts, the national food grains production, covering remaining production (i.e. approx 3%) of the country, will be 207.32 and 227.02 million tonnes in the year 2005-06 and 2010-11 respectively. The break up of cereals will be 193.18 and 212.01 million tonnes while the break up for pulses would be 14.13 and 15.01 million tonnes for the two time periods. In the year 2005-06, the National food grains requirement, covering remaining population (i.e approx. 3%) of the country, would be 213.21 with a break up of 193.38 million tonnes for cereals and 19.82 million tonnes for the pulses. By the year 2010-11, the national food grains requirement would be about 230.37 million tonnes with a break up of 209.00 for the cereals and 21.37 million tonnes for the pulses.

4.6 ASSESSMENT OF FOOD GRAINS STORAGE

As already estimated, the national food grains production will be 207.32 and 227.02 million tonnes in the year 2005-06 and 2010-11 respectively. On the basis of production and estimated marketed surplus ratio the marketed surplus of food grains would be about 123.56 and 135.31 million tonnes for the year 2005-06 and 2010-11. As the estimated storage requirement, in the present exercise, is based on seasonal and distribution approach and on this basis the storage requirement has been concluded about 54% of total marketed surplus of food grains i.e. maximum marketed surplus of a particular season. The approach is supported with the assumption that marketed surplus is distributed over the years and at the most the surplus would stay up to six months. The estimated storage requirement of food grains for the two periods is shown in Fig. 4.9.

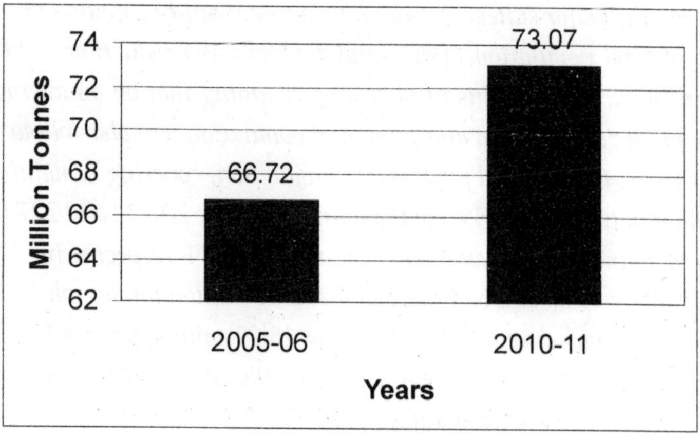

Fig. 4.9 National food grains storage requirement

The above storage requirement estimated only for food grains. Similarly, the requirement for oilseeds, sugarcane, cotton, spices, rubber, tea, coffee etc. can be estimated by developing the similar seasonal and distribution approach provided we have estimates of projections of production, Marketed Surplus Ratios and idea of distribution pattern of marketed surplus over the seasonal years for these crops. The idea of pattern of distribution of marketed surplus over the year is necessary to develop a realistic assumption.*

Note*—For example, the major oil seeds crops are groundnut, rapeseed and mustard and soybean which contributes nearly 84% of total oil seed production. The harvesting month of ground nut is November. Mustard is a major Rabi crop (sown during October-November and harvested during February-March). The harvesting month of soybean is Oct-Nov i.e. it coincides with the harvesting month of groundnut which together with soybean contributes about 60% of the production. It means the storage requirement is 60% of total marketed surplus. The data from 1995-96 to 2004-05 indicates that the Kharif oil seeds have always more than share of 60% of total oil seed production. Therefore storage capacity approximately equal to 60% of the total production of oilseeds is the safety point. Assuming that the produce normally stays for the 4 to 6 months the storage would be capable to maintain the rest of the production of Rabi Oil seeds crop.

For sugarcane, there is a need of separate storage because the storages developed for oilseeds and food grains will not have any space to carry the sugar because of busy cycle of oil seeds and food grains. The sugar harvesting period starts in Nov and at the most close in April. This is also the sugar mills operating time. It means the production distributes over the period from Nov to April or 5 months. Considering that the sugar at the most stays for 3 months than storage requirement is about 60% of produce.

Tea in southern India is harvested through out the year, but at longer intervals during the long and dry months (December to March). In northern India, the tea bush is plucked at weekly intervals from April to December and there is marked dormant season during winter when practically no crop is harvested. It can therefore be concluded that the mainly harvesting takes place from April to December i.e. 9 months or the produce is distributed over 9 months. The storage capacity is 1/9th of marketed surplus considering that a lot of produce stays for one month. The harvesting periods of various coffee producing countries are different as it is harvested during the dry season. In India it is November to February. It means the marketed surplus is distributed for four months. Considering that one lot of produce stays at the most for two months. The storage capacity is 1/2 of total marketed surplus.

CHAPTER 5

POLICY PLANNING AND IMPLICATIONS

The major conclusion which can be drawn from the analysis is that the Haryana, Punjab, Rajasthan, Madhya Pradesh and Uttar Pradesh will continue to be the backbone of food security of the country in the near future. The self sufficiency is observed in the case of cereals in the coming Eleventh Five Year Plan while the pulses will continue to be in the deficit situation. The food grains production to meet the requirement seems to be in deficit mainly due to stagnation in the production of pulses. The rising population has also be one of the factors to enlarge the deficit. As per the estimates, the production performance of cereals will not be adequate to meet the requirement in the Tenth Five Year Plan and therefore, the policy focus on the cereals production need to be continued along with the increase in the production of pulses to achieve the self sufficiency in the food grains. The liberalization regime propounds free trade and comparative cost advantage, which means diversion from food grain crops to profitable commercial crops. The cereals are the most important component in the food basket of food stuff and accounts for the largest part of energy supply in the diet. If the diversion is at the cost of cereal crops then the extent of diversion needs to be examined on the basis of food security levels and accordingly policy support may be determined for non-food crops.

A constructive policy and planning is very essential to achieve the food security in the long run. The planning of every state should be based on the local food habits and agricultural practices. Every state need to prevent imbalances in access to food, on the basis of social and economic classes, gender and age groups of people. It is also a primary responsibility of the state to facilitate food production commensurate with the population growth, physical and economic access to food through self-employment programmes and public distribution system. The policy issues dealing with food security for every state are very large. On the basis of present analysis and selected studies, it has been tried to cover some policies and planning implications and the same is given in the present chapter for the states selected in the study. However, the policy issues given for one state may also be applicable for another state depending upon the agricultural and social condition. The present chapter is divided into three sections. Section 5.1 is framed to present the policy implications for food grains surplus states. The policy planning implications for food grains deficit states is given in Section 5.2. Section 5.3 focuses on the common policy and planning for the states.

5.1 POLICY IMPLICATIONS FOR FOOD GRAIN SURPLUS STATE

The analysis indicated that in the year 2005-06, Punjab will be the largest food grains surplus state followed by the Haryana, Uttar Pradesh, Rajasthan and Madhya Pradesh. In 2010-11, the

Punjab will remain at first position as the food grains surplus state, followed by the Haryana, Rajasthan, Uttar Pradesh and Madhya Pradesh. The states of Haryana, Punjab, and Uttar Pradesh will continue to be food grains surplus states mainly because of the large availability of cereals. However, these states will continue to be in deficit in pulses. Therefore, there is need to expand the production of pulses either by increasing production or area or both. The states of Rajasthan and Madhya Pradesh will be in surplus in both cereals and pulses and have immense scope to increase the production of these crops due to large availability of land.

The policy implications for the food grains surplus states can be summarized as follows :

5.1.1 HARYANA

In the state of **Haryana**, it has been estimated that about 50 percent of total geographical area in the state is affected with the problems of alkalinity, salinity, water logging and soil erosion. A large part of total cultivable geographical area of the state is already under plough and there is very little scope to bring additional area under cultivation. In these situations, the degraded land should be reclaimed with proper soil conservation measures and fertility status of the soil should be maintained.

5.1.2 PUNJAB

The state of **Punjab** is deficit in pulses production and proper policy measures need to be adopted by increasing the area of HYV pulses crops. The research studies show that there is overcapitalization in agriculture sector of the state and capital assets are grossly underutilized due to small and decreasing size of farms. It increases the cost of production and hit the profitability of farm enterprises. These high costs may adversely affect the competitiveness in the international market. It has also been observed that the water is not used in efficient way and water table is falling every year. The south western districts in Punjab face problem of water logging and there is deceleration in growth rate of farm production and employment elasticity with respect to output. In these conditions the technology of production in the state needs to be improved along with changes in cropping pattern as it will be helpful to stabilize income and employment in the farming sector. Secondly, the water, which is a critical natural resource to determine the food security in the long run, should be used efficiently.

5.1.3 UTTAR PRADESH

The **Uttar Pradesh** is one of the major states of the Indian Union. The state of Uttar Pradesh is surplus in cereals production but deficit in pulses production. The growth of population is major problem and the declining per capita per day availability of food grains indicates that the population is comparatively increasing faster than the food grains production. Food security in the long run would partly depend on the slowing down of population growth rate in this state.With the increasing population, the per capita net sown area is further on the decline. The growth of the population which is mainly due to the change of demographic transition pattern from initial levels of high birth-rate high death rate to the intermediate transition stage of high birth rate–low death rate needs to be reduced by controlling high birth rates. It goes without saying that the country cannot make any significant progress and the growth in the country's economy would not be possible to the desired extent till this state remains backward. About 73% of total population is still dependent on agriculture for their livelihood, while the total share of the state's revenue from agriculture sector is near to 36%. In this way, approximately 64% of the states revenue is going to the 27% non-agricultural workers. According to the figures available for the year 1999-2000 by planning commission for the undivided state, as many as 31.15% people in Uttar Pradesh are living below the poverty line against the national average of 26.10%. Uttar Pradesh is a state where there is a tremendous scope for development through diversification. in the agricultural sector. The gross cropped area can also be increased considerably by increasing irrigation facilities.

5.1.4 MADHYA PRADESH

The state of **Madhya Pradesh** is self sufficient in food grains which are mainly due to introduction of High Yielding Varieties in the year 1964, development of suitable production technology and package approach for different crops, intensification of research for developing better H.Y Strains and creation of infrastructure to support production programmes. Apart from these positive features the state has many constraints like large tribal population, marginal and small farmers having low investment capacity for adoption of high technology, low cropping intensity due to practice of keeping land fallow in kharif and taking only one crop on residual/ conserved moisture in Rabi in some part of the state, high proportion of low value crops i.e. coarse cereals in cropping patterns, inadequate technological development suitable to specific regions of the state, particularly varieties suitable to match rainfall patterns. A large portion of the cultivated area in the state is rain fed and large proportion of cultivable waste and fallow land arising out of the rain fed agriculture and apart from this there are large turnoff and soil erosion problems in the state. The state can play the major role to provide the food security to the country if these constraints are removed. The main focus or the strategy should be to massive soil and water conservation measures through integrated watershed development programme, rationalization of cropping through the crop substitution in up land rice area and coarse cereals and wasteland development etc.

5.1.5 RAJASTHAN

Although, the state of **Rajasthan** is predominantly agrarian and surplus in food grains production but the drought has become the common feature of the state. The agricultural output is volatile and is dependent on the behaviour of the monsoon, therefore the irrigation potential needs to be increased. A large part of the geographical area in the state is waste and fallow land hence the necessary measures in agriculture sector should be taken so that waste and fallow land can be brought under cultivation. The food security in Rajasthan is mainly critical for drought affected districts and there is a need to take appropriate measures and to be precautious especially during this crisis period and those who are identified as vulnerable should be given drought rations. There should also be drought relief programmes and giving people food in return for their labour in these periods.

5.2 POLICY IMPLICATIONS FOR FOOD GRAIN DEFICIT STATES

The analysis reveals that in the year 2005-06, the state of Bihar will have the highest food grains deficit followed by the state of Maharashtra, Kerala, Tamil Nadu, Gujarat, West Bengal, Andhra Pradesh, Assam, Orissa, Karnataka, Jammu and Kashmir and Himachal Pradesh. In the year 2010-11, the state of Bihar will again have the highest food grains deficit followed by the state of Kerala, Maharashtra, Tamil Nadu, West Bengal, Gujarat, Andhra Pradesh, Orissa, Assam, Karnataka, Jammu and Kashmir and Himachal Pradesh. The policy implications for the food grains deficit states can be summarized as follows.

5.2.1 BIHAR

The state of **Bihar** is currently facing regional disparities, low yield of crops per hectare and declining capital formation. Besides, the state is also lacking action oriented policy programmes required to rejuvenate the agriculture sector. Therefore there is a need of dynamic agriculture policy in the state which should include the coverage of area by High Yielding Varieties of food grains and proper market, credit and extension services for the farmers to realize optimum potential of agriculture. The situation of food security in the state of Bihar is not encouraging and it becomes more worse when PDS system is not efficient.

5.2.2 MAHARASHTRA

In the state of **Maharashtra**, the studies related to the state indicates that the cropped area under food-grains has been going down with a simultaneous increase in the area under non-food grains such as sugarcane, cotton, etc. The extent of diversion needs to be examined on the basis of food security levels and proper measures need to be adopted. There are also evidences that the net shown area has been decreasing and land use pattern in Maharashtra also shows a shift towards increase in land towards non-agricultural use. With the increasing population and decreasing net sown area, the per capita availability of net sown area is further on the decline.

5.2.3 KERALA

Kerala is a food deficit state and due to trends in the decline of the area under rice cultivation and the continuing increase in the requirement as a result of population increase, this deficit is likely to go up in coming years. The state such as Kerala, which does not have much land for cultivation but has a large number of well-educated people, should emphasize biotechnological developments and evolution of High Yielding Varieties to increase the food grains production.

5.2.4 TAMIL NADU

In the state of **Tamil Nadu**, there is a diversion of land from agriculture to non-agriculture uses which adversely affects the growth in agriculture sector. The available land is also subjected to soil-erosion of varying degrees and degradation problems of different magnitudes The objective of agricultural development on an ecologically sustainable basis can be attained only when conservation, development and management of the land and water resources are assured. It has been reported in a policy note 2003-04 of agriculture department of Tamil Nadu that due to the pressures of urbanization, the net sown area declined from close to 60 lakh hectares to nearly 52 lakh hectares and gross cropped area declined from around 66 lakh hectares to about 62 lakh hectares during the period from 1990-91 to 2001-02. The ground water situation is also reported not very encouraging with in majority of the blocks. The water table shrinks when there is over exploitation of ground water at a rate much faster than the natural recharge.

The important measures needs to be adopted in the state are the soil conservation programmes along with development of waste land for cultivation purposes. There is also a need to increase the productivity through a package of irrigation management along with the proper use of the efficiency of water by promotion of micro irrigation structures like drip and sprinkler systems. The watershed is a hydrological unit and the water conservation and rainwater harvesting is said to be more effective when taken up as part of watershed management. The Watershed management should involve with soil and water conservation programmes integrated with appropriate cropping pattern, proper agricultural practices with the objective of improving the productivity, profitability and prosperity of the farmers.

5.2.5 GUJARAT

The state of **Gujarat**, recently, has faced natural calamities like drought and earthquakes. Early warning systems and monitoring of all meteorological, hydrological, and agricultural conditions are always helpful to tackle the situation of natural calamities in more effective manner. In the year 1999, insufficient and irregular rains during the expected monsoon season created drought situations. The UNICEF report on the situation in Gujarat indicates that more than 75% of the villages in Saurashtra in the west of Gujarat are suffering acutely from the drought, while conditions are not much better in Kutch. It has also been also feared that the situation may worsen in the remaining weeks of summer with the shortage of drinking water. The shortage of food may have adverse impact on the health of the drought victims particularly for the vulnerable group of women and children. Employment generation should be an integral part of drought management strategy of state government in drought affected areas. The situation of the drought is best tackled by a common approach of Watershed Management, which aims at overall development of the region along with measures for mitigation of droughts. It has been observed that in Saurashtra region of Gujarat, where soil fertility is high, the impact of watershed development by some NGO,s had a significant impact on the crop yields.

5.2.6 WEST BENGAL

The state of **West Bengal** ranks first in rice production, the fluctuation of which also affects the total cereals production. May to September for Aus, June to November to Aman and March to June for Boro rice are the three main rice seasons, out of which the Aman rice constitutes the largest proportion of area in the state. The stagnancy or fluctuations in growth of paddy has been observed in the state. The major factors identified are uneven distribution of rainfall and natural calamities. The state is prone to cyclones, droughts and floods which cause the loss in production.

There is a need to develop the Warning and Monitoring Systems in the state which would be helpful to prepare arrangements in advance to tackle the situation like drought, cyclones and other natural disasters in a more effective manner. Development of irrigation potential, improving water management system, and use of drought and water resistant varieties will be helpful to minimize the loss in production.

5.2.7 ANDHRA PRADESH

In the state of **Andhra Pradesh**, there is a need of balanced approach to grow food grains and cash crops. The comparison of different crops area from 1980-81 to 1995-96 indicates that the area of cotton has increased by many folds while area of Jowar has reduced drastically. In last two decades the area of Jowar is either changing into fallow lands or cotton producing lands.The rice has come as main food crop in the state in terms of food security and food supplies. The dependence on this food crop in some region, like telangana, can be observed because of its distribution by PDS in larger proportion which results in changing millet eating culture into rice eating culture. Jowar is a type of crop which demands very less input for the production and comparatively more nutritional value than the rice. Thus, this crop can help not only to provide food security but also nutritional security particularly to poor segment of population who is mainly dependent on cereals for their food security. There may be reform-dictated pressure in coming years to reduce the subsidy on welfare measures like PDS, and in these situations the poor farmers can be food secure only if they are self dependent in food crops by allocating the minimum area for these crops as per their needs.

5.2.8 ASSAM

The state of **Assam** is rich in diverse plant and animal genetic base and other natural resources like abundant rainfall, alluvial soil etc, but inspite of this fact the development of agriculture in the state has been slow over the decades. As a result, the state is lagging behind in comparison to many other states in the country and also unable to meet its own requirements in many agricultural commodities including food grains. It has been concluded from different studies that the system of farming in the state is still primitive and impact of modern science and technology in the state in modern farming is below the expected level. In hills, the century old system of shifting cultivation "Jhumming" is unable to even provide minimum level of standards to tribals, who are engaged in farming in hill districts. It is also seen that the yield levels of major foodgrains crops in Assam is low below their corresponding national averages. The irrigation level,which acts as a driving force in enhancing agricultural production, is also low. No doubt there are also few problems by nature in the state like the frequent occurrences of large scale floods in the state during the rains, comparatively greater water-logging in the areas and problems of Soil Conservation in the terrain of the hilly portion.On the food security point of view, there is a need to lower down the gap between food grains production and requirement in the state which can be possible through the cover the area from high yielding varieties where low yielding varieties are prevalent. The farmers in the state, specially in hill areas, should be given knowledge and trained in modern system of farming and agronomic practices through the extension programmes. The potential of irrigation needs to be increased in the state, as the irrigation is a base for intensive farming and major requirement for successful agriculture. The suitable agronomic practices are needed in parts of state where flood is problem.

5.2.9 KARNATAKA

In the state of **Karnataka**, rice, ragi and jowar are mainly grown for home consumption while maize and arhar (red gram) are produced mainly for the market. Ragi is a crop grown in southern Karnataka while Jowar is mainly in northern Karnataka. There is growth performance gap between ragi and jowar which is attributed mainly due to poor development status of northern Karnataka comparatively to southern Karnataka. The state ranks third in maize production in the country and its importance is due to the demand from the food processing and poultry feed industries. The arhar is cultivated as an intercrop in rain fed situations and the cost of cultivation of this crop is low. This crop does not expose the heavy losses to the farmer in the event of failure.

The policies needs to be concentrated on the infrastructure development of parts of the state where it is lacking. The evolution of the varieties of the food grains and other crops, suitable for drought and rain fed area, is essential to save the farmers in distress conditions. Growth promoting strategies like research, extension, credit and marketing along with proper insurance policies for these crops should be given attention on the priority basis.

Land and water are the two critical resources which should be considered for improvement for long term food security in the state. It has been observed that the continuing degradation of land and other factors poses a serious to sustained agricultural growth. The water resources are owing to over exploitation. A large part of the agriculture in state is also located in drought prone area. It has been estimated that about 26 percent of agricultural land at present is under irrigation while there are possibilities to increase the irrigation potential up to 45 percent. There is a need to expand this irrigation potential with proper exploitation policies for water.

5.2.10 HIMACHAL PRADESH

In the state of **Himachal Pradesh**, irrigation is one of the problems in the state and its potential can be increased through the rain water harvesting which may be helpful to provide irrigation to crops and recharging the ground water. The farm mechanization in reference to the hills also needs to be given thrust as it can reduce the cost of cultivation for the food grain crops. One of the limitations in this state is that the area under cultivation cannot be extended to the appreciable extent. Therefore in view to increase the production of food grains in the state, the research activities in the agricultural university should emphasize the evolution of High Yielding Varieties of food grains crop suitable for the state and this research should be extended to the farmers through the extension workers on the priority basis. In mid and low hills, Maize is the potential crop occupying largest area and production during Kharif season. The productivity level of this crop need to be increased from the present productivity level by introduction of high yielding hybrid varieties of maize. There is a need to develop this crop as a cash crop for the farmers of mid and low hills as well as maize based industry in these areas. The availability of marketing facilities, cheap credit and provision of agricultural inputs are very important for the development of agriculture and apart from governmental agencies, co-operative societies can also perform these functions.

5.2.11 ORISSA

In **Orissa**, agriculture, animal husbandry and fisheries are the major source of food security and the large majority of them dependent on agriculture for livelihood. Comparatively, the food security of the districts prone to cyclones is more critical. The strategy for food security needs to be focus on small, marginal farmers, landless wage earners and those who are under below poverty line as well as nutrition deficient, problematic and coastal areas which are prone to cyclones. The farm productivity, which may increase income and agricultural wages, should be increased. Besides there should be provision of additional off-farm and non-farm employment through different welfare and development programmes.

5.2.12 JAMMU AND KASHMIR

The state of **Jammu and Kashmir** is also deficit in food grains production therefore the main strategy of Jammu and Kashmir government is to achieve self-sufficiency and self-reliance in terms of production of food grains production. Increasing agricultural production through extension of irrigation should be a part of the basic agricultural strategy and underground water resources needs to be explored and exploited in the areas of the Jammu division where gravity schemes are not feasible. The productivity level of the food grains crop need to be increased from the present productivity level by introduction of high yielding varieties. The research activities in the agricultural university should emphasize the evolution of High Yielding Varieties of food grains crop suitable for the state and this research should be extended to the farmers through the extension workers on the priority basis. The farm mechanization in reference to the valley also needs to be given thrust as it can reduce the cost of cultivation for the food grain crops.

5.3 COMMON POLICY IMPLICATIONS

5.3.1 INCREASED FOOD AVAILABILITY

Food security at the national level is determined by the increased food availability therefore development of agriculture is the main issue beyond the food security. The growth rate in agricultural output is composed of growth rate in area and growth rate in yield. There are limits to increase the agricultural production through increase in area as land is a fixed factor of production. Naturally, increase in agricultural output will have to come almost wholly from growth in yield. As resources are dwindling, securing the nations food supply in the next decades is going to depend crucially on yield-increasing innovations. The cropping intensity should be increased by multiple harvests with the help of modern seed varieties and irrigation. There is a need for further research to improve the productivity of coarse food grains and pulses which can be grown in rain-fed areas. With the increasing population and decreasing net sown area, the per capita availability of net sown area is further on the decline. Growing population pressure and a diminishing resource base threaten food security in the coming century and there is no easy solution to increase food production. In these situations, yields will have to be improved through modern agricultural technology and scientific innovations. The fluctuations in food grains production seriously affect the food security. The challenge for the Indian agriculture that lies ahead is not only increase the agricultural production substantially but also to achieve stability in it. At the national level, there must be unique policy and planning frame work to eliminate food insecurity with the proper coordination of different ministries or departments and by combining the efforts of those who work in diverse sectors such as agriculture, nutrition, health, education, social welfare, economics, public works and the environment

In many states, it has been observed that the area under coarse cereals and per capita availability of pulses is falling. The coarse cereals eating culture in many areas is going to be changed as rice or wheat eating culture and due to this the per capita consumption of coarse cereals is declining. A reduction in per capita availability of pulses adversely affects the protein intake. As a substitute, if coarse cereal is provided to poorest segment than it will be comparatively inexpensive and improve calorie intake.

5.3.2 PHYSICAL AND ECONOMIC ACCESS

The availability of food is essential but is not a sufficient condition for the household and individual food security i.e. there should be the physical access for food accompanied by economic access. The physical access and economic access is always analyzed in respect of Public Distribution Systems and poverty levels of the household respectively, therefore the establishment of an efficient Public Distribution System (PDS) and eradication of household poverty are also the important considerations to achieve the food security.

The PDS has its origin during the Second World War period and has been an important source for enhancing the food security for the poor. Under the PDS, the Central Government ensures the supply of essential commodities to the state government, and these items are distributed through a network of retail outlets known as fair price shops. A revised scheme for distribution known as Targeted Public Distribution System has also been introduced in late nineties. One of the distinctive features of the Targeted PDS in relation to previous policy in India is the division of the entire population into below-poverty-line (BPL) and above-poverty-line (APL) categories, based on the poverty line defined by the Planning Commission. Another distinguishing feature is that the PDS now has dual central issue prices: prices for BPL consumers and prices for APL consumers. A efficient Public Distribution System is a essential component of any country to improve food security, as some states may not produce enough food for all the people. The reason is that the natural resources, population, and agricultural production technologies are distributed unevenly around the states.

It is a well established fact when the resources (especially land) and technology constraints limit the aggregate food production its negative impact on food security can be seen not only on household but also at state, regional and national level.

Food security for the nation as a whole is a separate thing. If we look at food security for individual states, we may find that the picture is not as good. Also, the adequacy of food grains at state level does not guarantee the availability of food grains at household level until and unless distribution is proper and there is no constraints of purchasing power for the poor segment of population. This is particularly true for the segment of population living below the poverty line and unable to get two meals in a day or facing hunger. In other words, this population segment faces the situation of food insecurity due to under nourishment.

The definition of 'poverty' varies from country to country and several economists and organizations have given different estimates of poverty. The norm given by the expert group of Planning Commission defined poverty line on the basis of nutritional norm of per capita daily intake of 2400 calories in rural areas and 2100 calories for urban areas. A person who fails to obtains this minimum level calories is being treated as below the poverty line. Data provided by the planning commission indicates that in 1999-2000, there is about 26.10% of population in our country below the poverty line. It means that more than 26.10% of the population in India is facing food insecurity or earns less than what it takes to access the barest essentials of life. Among the major states, the highest poverty ratio is observed in Orissa (47.15%) followed by Bihar (42.60%), Madhya Pradesh (37.43%), Assam (36.09%), Uttar Pradesh (31.15%), Maharashtra(25.02%), West Bengal(27.02%), Karnataka (20.04%), Tamil Nadu (21.12%), Andhra Pradesh (15.77%), Rajasthan (15.28%), Gujarat (14.07%), Kerala(12.72%), Haryana (8.74%),Himachal Pradesh (7.63%), Punjab (6.16%), Jammu and Kashmir (3.78%). In these circumstances the Public Distribution System, which is one of the most important instruments in providing food security at household level, should be efficient along with the development of programmes in which the surplus food grains can be used as wage goods.

Poverty is an evil and its eradication is very essential to maintain peace and achieve sustainable development. The poor segment of population or the population below the poverty line may be very constructive if supported with employment programmes and destructive in case if face the situation of hunger. In our country there is wide income inequalities and there is heavy concentration of income in the hands of few people. This rich section has to make a greater effort in the process of growth with realization that no society can grow without the help of other section or society irrespective of the income status and their role need to be concentrated to provide maximum employment creation to other sections of society giving due weightage to the poor segment of population.

One main condition to provide food security *via* Public Distribution System is a constructive political leadership that is responsive and think by heart for the poor people. The efficacy of any food security system at household level and individual level can be judged only with reference to the Public Distribution System through which it is translated into action. The state like Kerala has been a successful in respect of universal coverage of the PDS which provided access to food grains for the majority of population. The states are supposed to be adversely affected due to the shift in the uniform food policy, in the late nineties. The reason is that while the intention of the Targeted PDS is to provide benefits to the poor, the outcome may not be satisfactory on account of many problems in identifying the "poor". It is possible that the APL category may includes even agricultural laborers and farmers. Therefore, it is necessary againto reintroduce a universal Public Distribution System for consumers not only in state but throughout the country with uniform central issue prices for the food grains distributed through the PDS.

It is also necessary that the PDS should have wide coverage and secondly, it should be without any leakage. The PDS can effectively target poor, if linked through employment programmes or food for work programme but one of the limitations of such programme is that it could not be targeted to large section of poor people. A system can true to the people only if the procedures and way of working is transparent and the other way to make the system efficient in this process is to cross check and series of inspection with in the organizations involved in food security programmes at grassroot level.

A good procedure may have the following steps to make the PDS effective.

(1) The items distributed through PDS should be sold in packing and not in open manner. The packing should bear note that the items are for PDS and not for open sale.

(2) These items should be packed on the basis of grades for the PDS framed by the particular agency and this agency should have the powers to check the packed items by taking the samples at random from the market. This step will also ensure the quality in PDS items.

(3) These PDS essential items should be purchased by PDS Stamps (or coupons) which may be supplied either through employment programmes or school childrens. Every PDS stamp should bear No., Price, Quantity to be supplied and other required information's. In this way the Public Distribution System will also have the wide coverage.

(4) In the era of privatization and globalization, every state Government should also allow to keep the essential distribution items in all General Stores (Shops), NGOs etc. which is to be directly supplied by an agency involved in food security programmes as it will raise the competition with allotted Fair Price Shops and ultimately raise the efficiency of system. The commission may be given to store keepers to keep and distribute these essential items through the PDS Food stamps. Again, on behalf of collected PDS stamps, the Govt. should issue the essential items to the shop keepers and other agencies responsible for distribution.

The 'right to food' and 'right to life' are closely interlinked and PDS determines right to food for the poor people to the large extent. It can be possible to reduce the starvation deaths of poor people by the efficient management of PDS.

5.3.3 WARNING AND MONITORING SYSTEMS

Early warning, including close monitoring of all meteorological, hydrological, and agricultural conditions should be established throughout the country. This helps in preparing arrangements in advance to tackle the situation like drought, cyclones and other natural disasters in a more effective manner. Employment generation should be the integral strategy of drought and natural disasters management for the government through the arrangement of special funds. The arrangements to combat the drought and other natural disasters should include the planning for health, access of food grains to the needed people, drinking water and fodder supply during the drought or other natural disasters period. Once drought is declared in particular region, the revenue collection, loans recovery needs to be suspended and assistance should be provided for crop damage, damage to animal husbandry, along with the immediate starting of food for work programme. The states like Orissa and West Bengal which are prone to famines and crop failures needs to frame proper stock holding policies maintaining a minimum safe level of basic cereal stock for the people. The stocks should be located at place which optimize the financial cost involved in transportation and also facilitate urgent shipment to recipient places in the shortest possible time.

5.3.4 DEVELOPMENT OF FOOD INSECURITY AND VULNERABILITY INFORMATION AND MAPPING SYSTEMS (FIVIMS)

FIVIMS is essentially a database involving network of information and mapping system, which assembles detailed information about the people who are food insecure and their location.

Recently, FAO and Ministry of Agriculture on behalf of Government of India have signed a Pilot Project for Developing National Food Insecurity and Vulnerability Information and Mapping System in India in the two states *viz.* Himachal Pradesh and Orissa. The other states also needs to be covered to develop the FIVIMS in the country and the preference should be given for states having higher poverty ratio to lower poverty ratio. The development of relevant data base should be first for drought and flood affected districts with in the states.

5.3.5 STABILIZATION OF POPULATION

Agriculture being the most important segment of Indian Economy and it has always been given the highest priority by the Government. The growing Scientific and Technological revolution in the field of agriculture has expanded the production, enhanced farm productivity and net return per unit of area investment. In India, rapid population growth rate making difficult for agricultural production to keep pace with the rising requirement for food. Therefore, a primary condition for food security is stabilization of population.i.e. achieving food security in the long run depends on the slowing down of population growth rate. Due to high population growth and consequent pressure on land, the per capita land holding in India is decreasing. This population pressure has led to subdivision and fragmentation of holdings, disguised unemployment in agriculture and marginal productivity of land which is zero and even negative in some regions.

In almost all the states, population growth has become the major problem and many states already are cultivating most of the arable land under cultivation. There are also evidences that the land use pattern in major states also shows a shift of cultivable area towards non-agricultural use. The country like our nation which have high population growth should regenerate their resource base and achieve a sustained social transformation.

The rate of growth of population is a function of birth rate and death rate. Demographic transition is a global phenomenon and changes in population growth and pattern of age profile of the population are inevitable during the transition. In India, the growth of the population is mainly due to the changes in demographic transition pattern from initial levels of high birth rate - high death rate to the intermediate transition stage of high birth rate - low death rate. The recent trends on population growth confirms that the success of population policy will largely depend on the performance of four major states, Bihar,

Madhya Pradesh, Rajasthan and Uttar Pradesh (BIMARU States).

Human development and improvement in quality of life has been the ultimate objectives of almost in all plannings. It is a matter of great concern that nearly 50 years of planned development has failed to initiate any retardation in India's population, despite the fact that India is the first country to adopt the national population control programme in 1952. The successful implementation of National Population Control Policy depends on the involvement of local people, honest working of medical department and district administration. An unnecessary birth has very strong correlation with the educational level of the mother and reduction of this birth is the imperative need of family planning programme or family welfare programme. The educated women's and other members of the panchayat in the rural areas should be involved in population control programme because the net working comprising women's can only understand the nature and problems of women's related to rural areas secondly, the family size is largely determined by level of education and the spread of literacy among the women's.

In designing the family welfare programmes, every thing should not be concluded from the statistical analysis i.e. things should be observed to identify that where is problem. One problem is that the many people have less faith on sterilisation provided by family planning/ welfare staff at the health centres. Therefore, a large part of the success of family welfare programmes depends on the use of contraceptives.

Like PDS the family welfare programmes should also have wide coverage. As, it has already been stated that a birth is strongly correlated with the educational level of the mother i.e. a educated mother can avoid the unnecessary birth and vice versa. The education is linked with poverty levels and the people who are below the poverty line are in general deprived of education due to many factors and is largely responsible for high birth rate. As given, this section also needs PDS facility and contraceptives can therefore be distributed to the mother of a poor family along with in the covered packets of PDS items. In this way, the family welfare and food security objectives can be integrated to get the desired results.

5.3.6 WOMEN'S ROLE IN FOOD SECURITY

The ultimate goal of agricultural research is to benefit farmers. These benefits can be more realized if women in developing country like India can be involved in policy-making and planning to ensure the most productive and efficient use of land and water resources to meet present and future food and agricultural demands, especially in areas of crop production and biodiversity. It has been felt that the agricultural extension services are not adequately covering the rural women and therefore participation needs to be increased to ensure the development and adequate transfer of technologies. Studies have shown a direct correlation between increased incomes for women and improvements in household food security and there fore women's participation in decision-making is fundamental to their role in development and contribution to food security. At work place, women should be given equal employment opportunities and competitive wages.

5.3.7 SCHOOL FEEDING PROGRAMMES

The major nutrition public health problems are, chronic energy deficiency and under-nutrition, Micro-nutrient deficiencies, Anaemia due to iron and folate, Vitamin A deficiency and Iodine Deficiency Disorders. Low dietary intake is the most important cause of under nutrition in children. SCHOOL feeding programmes are useful ways to ensure that the food insecure children have sufficient energy to concentrate on their studies and to combat under nutrition. These programmes not only improves the educational status and combat under nutrition of food insecure children but also helps to reduce the gender inequalities by increasing the participation of girls in education.

5.3.8 FOOD SUBSIDY AND FOOD SECURITY

In the era of globalization, there is always a pressure from developed countries on the developing countries to cut down the subsidies including food subsidies which is a kind of threat to food security of many people living in developing countries. The reduction of food subsidies raises the PDS prices of essential items and effect is always seen on people below the poverty line and its consequences are hunger, malnutrition, infant and neo-natal mortality and deaths due to starvation. For example in many parts of the country, particularly Orissa, are stalked by death due to starvation. The issue of food subsidy is therefore should not be linked to political or the foreign trade but it should be decided by the organisation at the international level like Food and Agriculture Organisation of the United Nations. At the international level, a range of specialized agencies and development organizations must work together as partners in a common effort to achieve the objective of global food security. Concerns about lagging agricultural production and rapid population growth, as well as inadequate food distribution systems, should be managed with the help of international organizations.

5.3.9 REDUCTION OF POST HARVEST LOSSES

It is estimated that about 10% of the food grains produced in the country is lost annually in harvesting, defective storage and ignorance of scientific operations (post harvest losses) before it reaches to the consumer. It means that about 20 million tonnes of food grains is lost after the post harvest operations which can feed millions of hungry people. These losses should be minimized. One effective way to reduce the post harvest losses is to make aware the correct stage of harvesting of food grains crops secondly the farmers should be trained in handling, packing and scientific operations of storages for the commodities.

5.3.10 MANAGEMENT OF WATER RESOURCES

Water is the primary necessity for the living creatures and plants and its proper management will have a direct influence on food security in India in the long run. With rapidly growing population, demands on water for domestic supplies, irrigation and industry, may lead to wide-spread inter-state conflicts. In our country there are regional variations in the rainfall and its pattern is uneven. The domination of the South-west monsoon in the making of India's climate results in wide spatial and temporal variations. The numbers of rainy days is least in Rajasthan and highest in Northeastern India. In case of excess rainfall there is flood in many parts while on the other hand, deficit in rainfall in some parts leads to doughty situation.

One of the effective ways to reduce regional imbalance and mitigate floods or droughts is to transfer the water from the surplus area to deficit areas which can be possible by the interlinking of rivers. The proposal for interlinking of the rivers in India has been prescribed at the national level to the local as the solution for addressing the twin problems of monsoon floods and water scarcity. The interlinking of rivers will raise the irrigation potential which may further helpful to increase the food production. By connecting the surplus rivers with those in the drier western and southern parts of the country, the proposed interlinking of rivers plan will be helpful to solve the twin problems of floods and water scarcity. It has been observed that the areas falling under the rivers like Brahmaputra and Ganga, particularly their northern tributaries, are surplus in water resources while large areas in the states of Rajasthan, Gujarat, Andhra Pradesh, Karnataka and Tamil Nadu face the recurring droughts. The project therefore needs to be developed to interlink the flood prone areas to doughty areas by the rivers and there should be proper strategy for water resources management by promoting equitable distribution and its judicious use, for the benefit of the local communities.

Watershed development is also one of the method to conserve the rain water. The network of farm ponds can be helpful in reducing the soil and nutrient loss, supply of water for protective irrigation, and recharging the ground water table. The modern technologies like Geographic Information System and Remote Sensing can be helpful in locating the areas for the watershed development.

5.3.11 INTEGRATED SOIL HEALTH AND PEST MANAGEMENT

The heavy use of fertilizers leads to the depletion of soil fertility. In India, the standard ratio for the use of Nitrogen, Phosphorous and Potassium has been assumed as 4:2:1. The ratio was estimated in the year 1998-99 at 8.5:3.1:1 which is highly imbalanced and consumption is biased in favour of nitrogenous fertilizer. This imbalance has lead to deterioration of soil health in major states.

There is a need to introduce a comprehensive fertilizer policy which should encourage the balanced fertilizer use in the country. The government should encourage the use of phosphatic and potassic fertilizers as well as other required micronutrients. It should be supported with a network of reliable soil testing facilities at block level. There should also be adequate policy support for promotion of eco-friendly technologies and use of Nutritional Supplements-farmyard manure, green manuring, vermicomposting and biofertilisers. The approach should be integrated with the pest management with the objective to control insect pests effectively and without any adverse after affects. This combined approach i.e. **"Integrated soil health and pest management"** should be implemented with the help of educated local farm youths and for this purpose there should be comprehensive planning to provide the training and employment. Implementation of this eco friendly approach would not only be helpful to maximize the crop production on sustainable basis but also may be helpful to reduce the migration of rural youth from rural to urban area in search of employment. The use of bio-fertilizers and bio-pesticides is essential for promoting and sustaining organic farming in the country. At present, the global market for organic food is on the rise and our country also needs to capture a major share.

5.3.12 TRADE LIBERALIZATION AND FOOD SECURITY

Trade liberalization has opened up several opportunities but there are also challenges. The opening up of Indian agriculture to trade boosted the demand and diversion of area towards non-food crops. The thrust on exports of agricultural produce has resulted in a significant change in cropping patterns in the country. Agricultural trade liberalisation has led to commercialisation of agriculture and a shift in cultivation away from food crops to cash crops. Indian producers have been diverting more and more cultivable land from food grains and pulses to the production of oilseeds, cotton, horticultural crops, prawn culture, animal husbandry etc. As a result, the area under food grain cultivation was declined in 1990's. Although, total agricultural output still rose during the 1990s, but the growth rate of food grains had been close to the population growth rate which implies stagnant per capita production level. In this way, the trade liberalisation reversed the process of recovery of per capita food availability, undermining the food security of the country. Simultaneously, it is always argued by the economists that the liberalization of import policy is driven not by the needs of the millions of workers and peasants who produce the commodities that are traded. The cutting down of import duties and placing of the particular agricultural commodity under the OGL brings the prices down and producers are adversely affected. The farmers always divert their cultivable area towards the cash crops in the impression that they will fetch higher prices but instead sometimes get low returns which affect their food security level. One of the reason of this lower return is the inability of farmers to understand the supply and demand dynamics in the era of liberalization. The "contract farming" may be helpful in this regard and therefore it should be permitted in every part of the country.

5.3.13 COMMODITY EXCHANGES AND FOOD SECURITY

Commodity exchanges are institutions which provide a platform for trading in 'commodity futures' just as how stock markets provide space for trading in equities and their derivatives. The future market provides a way for price discovery and risk management with the help of forecast of likely demand and supply of prices at a future point of time. The Government of India in 2003-04 had initiated major steps towards introduction of futures trading in commodities, which included removal of prohibition on futures trading in all the commodities by issue of a notification and setting up of the National Level Commodity Exchanges. It might be a right step to change the present unorganized and inefficient physical commodity market to national level structured and transparent market, but side by side there are also serious implications too.

The commodity exchanges had been claiming impressive growth in the volume of trade, the exact impact on the farmers needs to be assessed. The delivery is very low in commodity exchanges as the delivery is optional in commodity exchanges. The Futures Market is primarily intended for hedging but speculation is also coming as common feature in the markets. The negative aspect in this process is speculation which is encouraged by optional nature of delivery. The positive aspect is that it encourages also hedging which is a tool of risk management. The forward trading system which facilitates speculation and hoarding needs to be checked by an active and vigilant market watch and government policy measure need to promote a smoothly regulated market institution and to make provisions for investigation, enforcement and penalty in case of violations. There is a urgent need to develop set of regulations by market regulator Forwards Markets Commission (FMC) to ensure that a single player does not dominate the market and distort market forces as it may create inflationary pressures. With the coming up of commodity exchanges, there is also need to develop the parallel institutions to update the farmers about WTO, subsidies and pricing trend. These institutions should also help farmers in planning their farming in tune with domestic as well as international climate for the purpose to reduce the distress sale.

The commodity exchanges may be helpful to empower rural India *via* reducing the exploitation of farmers but in any system, there are also certain leakages which cannot be ignored. These leakages needs to be tapped at the initial planning level otherwise the adverse situation for farmers would like to be the same as it is going at present in the case of regulated market setup in the country. Besides filling these leakages the planning for a good system needs to concentrate on the point that in future what can be negative with our farmers and other sections of population irrespective of the fact that it is happening at present or not. It is also essential for the commodity exchanges to be successful in the long run. In India, there are evidences that the prices of these commodities may be less volatile in post on line trading period suggesting that the comparatively less price fluctuations would be helpful in stabilizing the income of farmers and deciding the cropping pattern of crops. But the issue is that how much extent the farmers has been benefited and is it due to real price discovery. Secondly, it has been observed that there has been inflationary trends in essential commodities like wheat, vegetables etc in post on line period which is harmful from the food security point of view as it affects mainly the land less labourers and low income urban population. Although, in addition to economic facts there may be many other factors for the price rise *viz* rise of population, decreasing productivity etc but the commodity exchanges also needs to check their role and one of the way for the commodity exchanges might be to allow the futures contract for the essential commodities only in the pre sowing period which in real sense would be helpful in deciding the cropping pattern on the basis of realistic demand or to match supply and demand. The second solution may be to impose an upper limit on future contracts in specific essential commodities.

The crucial question before the economists is to determine this limit for the essential food crops in a open economy in balanced manner providing economic safety to farmers on one hand and protecting the consumers on the other. The limit should not lead inflationary spiral, although a creeping or mild inflation in economy may be permitted. With a key watch on inflation, priority to protect the farmers always would be the safer side as it is also beneficial for the national economy and consumers in the long run. The reason is that if limit is imposed instantaneous and unfavorable to the farmers, then farmers might be affected economically in the current year and consequently will shift the acreage of food crops to other crops affecting consumers in next year. The farmers constitute the major population and rural work force of the country and raising the income of the same means raising the aggregate demand of industrial goods which in turn would increase the national income and employment as the enough productive capacity is available. The rise in aggregate demand would raise the profit of industries/firms due to increasing supply of the units of output. Besides, the initial level inflation due to rise in aggregate demand is also helpful to raise the profit of the industries/firms as prices of goods produced by the industries rise relatively faster than the cost of production because wages always lags behind the prices of goods. The sufferers due to this starting inflation are those who receive relatively the fixed income. As the income elasticity of demand for food is very high among the low income groups which is associated with the undernourishment, therefore, side by side, the instant policy measure related to food security includes the announcement of the optimum wages/allowances for laborers/employees and raise food subsidy through the welfare schemes to withstand the inflationary pressures in the food items and political instability. The estimated tax addition i.e. inflation tax, due to the increment of profit of these industries/firms should be allocated to increase the food subsidy.

One of the possible important leakages is the jacking up the prices purposively both the futures as well as spot prices prior to expiry of the contracts which can be created after taking the advantages of limited supply of the commodities by the big operators of trading houses, therefore, all the commodities may not be fit for futures trading. It has been observed that the highly volatile trends witnessed in spot markets just before and immediately after the expiry of futures contracts of commodities with small market size. These trends, particularly in spot market, are beyond the logic of any normal trading practices, especially when there is no significant increase in demand. As a result, this has been accruing huge losses to small traders in futures as well as in spot markets and the processors who operate for normal profit margins. Futures markets, aimed at price discovery and price risk minimization processes, are actually sending wrong signals to spot markets and turning them more volatile for commodities having small market.

A well developed spot market is a precondition for any commodity to be successful in Future Trading. The future markets is said to perform the economic functions of price discovery and price risk management. The price discovery is through the basic forces of supply and demand in spot and future markets. The commodity exchanges should be more transparent that how the prices are discovered or how these institutions are maintaining demand and supply curves to clear any doubtful situations. A more efficient regulatory mechanism need to be developed that facilitates smooth functioning of futures markets towards their core objectives of real price discovery and risk minimisation.

The extent of the positive or negative role and necessary requirements of the commodity exchanges needs to be analyzed *via* conducting the studies and it should be mandatory for the commodity exchanges to make transparent all the data like address of registered traders, intermediaries and institutions, clearly mentioning their margins and other related data on website, which are required for the study. The commodity exchanges has very initial setup and these institutions might be facing infrastructural requirement and several other bottlenecks for their operations. Therefore, in case of their positive role in the interest of nation, there is a need to facilitate these institutions *via* providing necessary infrastructure and to remove the bottlenecks for their successful operations and to create a transparent spot market.

5.3.14 POLICIES FOR FARMERS TO MAINTAIN THE FOOD SECURITY

The prosperity of the farmers, the builders of the nation, is very essential to maintain their food security and rest of the nation. There are reports that farmers are committing suicides mainly under the pressure of very high indebtedness and failure of repayment of their loans. The failure of repayment of loans is closely linked to repeated crop failures and inability to meet the rising cost of cultivation. The increasing cost of the cultivation of crops due to higher input prices increase the demand for the cash. The price of the produce does not increase correspondingly which affects the viability of farming. The crop failure is mainly due to natural calamities (insufficient rains, failure of monsoons, floods, drought etc), little or absence of irrigation in that area, reduction in productivity of land due to overuse of fertilizers and pesticides, excess rely on hybrid seed/ genetically modified seed or failure of germination of seed, susceptibility of crop to a large variety of pests and diseases etc. The farmers residing in the area facing these problems always face the cyclical crop failures which completely break the economic prosperity of farmers. The most dominant man made factor responsible to increase the intensity of crop failure is the "reduction in productivity of land due to overuse of fertilizers and pesticides" which needs to be discouraged *via* encouraging alternative low cost organic farming. There is a need to establish soil testing laboratories in the different parts of country and a comprehensive crop insurance scheme which would be helpful to prevent the suicides of farmers. The scheme needs to be designed in such a way so as to support minimum life support system *via* providing at least the cost of cultivation to the farmers in the case of crop failures. Agricultural trade liberalisation has led to commercialisation of agriculture and a shift in cultivation away from food crops to cash crops like oilseeds, cotton and horticultural crops etc. For example, it is reported that a significant area of land was diverted from food grains to cotton between 1991 and 1996. The cotton prices started declines from 1995-96 to 2001 due to increase in cotton imports at the low import duty (about 5%) which were allowed under the WTO treaties lifting the quantitative restrictions. In this way farmers suffered and only textile industry enjoyed *via* claiming that the cheaper imported cotton is better suited to the export requirements of Indian Textile Mills. In the state like Maharashtra, the cotton farmers have been protected to some extent by the state Unique Monopoly Cotton Procurement Scheme (MCPS) which is only assurance of a fair price of this cash crop. This type of schemes needs to be continue. The root of this problem can also be solved by changing economic and other policies in the line of dynamics of trade liberalization.

The volatility of crop prices has been a major source of income instability and distress for farmers. Prices often bear no relation to state-level or national output trends and sharp fluctuations in crop prices over the years also provide misleading signals to farmers, who tend to have high price response in terms of deciding the acreage under different crops. The price volatility faced by farmers becomes more sharper when there is insufficient procurement at announced MSP or completely mismatch between MSP and Cost of Cultivation. In the era of liberalization, the MSP should be alien much more closely to market price. This type of competitive structure of price for procurement would be helpful to reduce the dependency on imports for food security requirements.

The efforts should be made to develop new projects for surface water irrigation development, water shed development particularly in rain fed areas and control on overexploitation of ground water in areas having plenty of ground water resources.

In agricultural marketing, the farmers and producers are often disadvantaged due to their poor logistical connectivity, lack of awareness, ignorance about the potential of their produce, urge for quick liquidity credit, inputs availability, marketing and scientific storage.

The connectivity needs to be improved by building rural roads, specially connecting major production areas, which will help the farmers to minimize the losses in transportation and reducing the cost of transport/communication. Information on current prices, consumer changing preferences and demand etc. should receive the particular attention which may be given to farmers through websites, rural kiosks and mobile phones or any digital information technology as, now a days, the same is coming as cheaper mode of communication. The information should be provided on the basis of comparative advantages for each region for the different crops to get the maximum returns.

The urge for quick liquidity of credit can be solved by setting up of ware houses with grading facilities and the farmers may use the deposit receipt, obtained from warehouse after storing his produce, for credit to their account. Once the commodities are deemed negotiable and transferable, the warehouse receipts can be an effective tool in the hands of farmers. To encourage and assist farmers to use warehouse receipts banks can provide loans against receipts which are obtained against physical produce. This approach would also help the farmers in reducing the indebtness burden and the banking industry must come forward to help the farmers. The credit linkage under the warehouse storage will also help the banking industry to expand their agricultural credit. In addition the farmers should be able to avail pledge finance from commercial banks, APMC etc. and sell their produce when the market conditions are favorable.

An increase in the farmers share is taken as an evidence of increase in the efficiency of the marketing system and the farmer is benefited in this case and decrease in the farmers share is an evidence that middleman retain a larger share which is against the farmer. In order to protect the interest of farmers, there is a need to develop the marketing infrastructure to improve the marketing efficiency *via* reducing the cost of marketing and middleman's in marketing channel. In addition, the policies at state level should include the removal of restrictions on the movement of agricultural commodities and to ensure that the farmers receive prices commensurate with their efforts and investment. The farmers should be free to sell their produce anywhere and the structure of taxes on food grains and other crops needs to be rationalized.

The scientific storage needs to be developed with better techniques with a view to reducing post harvest losses and ensuring a better return to the farmer. Over period of time, the government is encouraging the increase storage capacity through various schemes with provision of subsidy. The scientific storage capacity should be created near to production areas so that the produce may come in storage in shortest possible time. The increasing density of godowns would be helpful for the farmers in easy accessibility for storing their produce which reduce their transportation cost and minimize post harvest wastages.

REFERENCES

***Achen, C.H. 1982.** Interpreting and Using Regression. California, Sage Publications. Breverely Hills, pp. 58-67.

Achyra, K.C.S., 1983. Food Security System of India, New Delhi. Concept Publications House.

Achyra, S.S., 2003. Agril. Marketing in India (as a Part of Millinium Study of Indian Farmers), p. 134.

Agril Statistics at a Glance 2001. Agricultural Statistics Division, Directorate of Economics and Statistics, Ministry of Agriculture, New Delhi.

Ahluwalia, Deepak (1993). Public Distribution of Food in India : Coverage, Targeting and Leakages : Food Policy, 8 (1), pp. 33-54

Ashok, R., 1969. Measurement in Economics, Calcutta. Allied Publishers, p. 37.

Bhagavati J and Srinivasan T.N. (1993). India's Economic Reforms, Ministry of Finance, Government of India, New Delhi.

Bhatia, M.S. 1999. Rural Infrastructure and Growth in Agriculture, Economic and Political Weekly, 34 (13) : A43-A48.

Brown, R.G. 1962. Smoothing Forecasting and Prediction of Discrete Time Series, New York, prentice Hall.

***Cameron, S. 1993.** Why is R^2 adjusted reported? Journal of Quantitative Economics, 9 (1) : 183-186.

Census of India 1991. Series 1 (India). Primary Census Abstract (General Population).

Chiney, S., 1993. Food Credit. Bank of India Monthly Review, 32 (12) : 666-674

Dahia, P.S. 1998. Food Security-Key Issues and Strategies, State Bank of India Monthly Review, 37 (2) : 78-93

Dhar, U.R., Berek, P. and Bigman, D. 1993. Management of India's Food Policy in the Coming Decade.

***FAO, 1983.** Report of the Eighth Session of the Committee on World Food Security, CL83/10 Rome 33 pp.

FAO, 1996. Rome Declaration on World Food Security and World Food Summit Plan of Action. World Food Summit 13-17 November 1996, Rome.

***FAO, 2002.** The State of Food Insecurity in the World 2001. Rome.

Frontline. The Roots of Tragedy, 32(14), July 2005.

George, P.S. 1994. Food Security in South Asia, Performance and Prospects. Economic and Political Weekly, 29 (18) : 1092-1094.

George, P.S. 1996. Public Distribution System, Food Subsidy and Production Incentives. Economic and Political Weekly, 31 (39) : A140-A144.

George, P.S. 1999. Some Reflections on Food Security in India. An Annual Conference of Indian Society of Agricultural Economics, 59th, Jabalpur, 1-3 December, 1999, pp 4-21.

Ghosh, M. 1998. Agrarian Structure and Rural Poverty in India. Journal of Contemporary Asia, 28 (2) : 175-184.

***Goldberger, A.S. 1991.** A Course in Econometrics, Massachusetts, Harvard University Press, Cambridge.

Gopalappa D.V. and Rao, V.M. 2004. Agricultural Growth and Farmer Distress : Tentative Perspectives from Karnataka, Economic and Political Weekly, Vol. 39, No. 52, Dec 25-31, pp. 5591-5593.

Government of India, Planning Commission, 2001. Report of the Working Group on Crop Husbandry, Demand & Supply Projections and Agricultural Inputs for the Tenth Five Year Plan, September, 2001, p. 45.

***Gragner, C. and New Bold, P. 1976.** R^2 and the Transformation of Regression Variables. Journal of Econometrics, Vol. 4, 205-210.

Gujrati, N.D., 1978. Basic Econometrics, New York, Mc Graw Hills.

Gupta, S.C. and Kapoor V.K. 1999. Fundamental of Mathematical Statistics, New Delhi, Sultan Chand and Sons.

Gupta, S.P. 1996. Statistical Methods, New Delhi, Sultan Chand and Sons.

Hanumantha R.C.H.; Radhakrishna, R.; Peters, G.H. and Braun, J. 1999. National Food Security : A Policy Perspective for India. An International Conference of Agricultural Economists on Food Security, Diversification and Resource Management : Refocusing the Role of Agriculture, 23rd, California, 10-16th August, 1999. Proceedings, pp. 77-96.

Hanumantha Rao, C.H., 1993. Agricultural Growth and Rural Poverty in India : Emerging Trends and Perspectives. Indian Economic Review. 28 (2) : 129-140.

ICMR, 1984. Recommended Dietary Intakes for Indians. New Delhi, ICMR Offset Press.

India Various Years. Ministry of Finance. Economic Division, Economic Survey, New Delhi, Government of India Press.

Indira, M. 1996. Structural Adjustment Policies and Rural Poor : Accessibility to Food and Vulnerability to Price Changes. Journal of Rural Development, 15 (1) : 1-12.

Indrakanth, S. 1997. Coverage and Leakages in PDS in Andhra Pradesh. Economic and Political Weekly, 32 (19) : 999-1001.

Johnson, L.A. and Montagomary, C.D. 1976. Forecasting and Time Series Analysis. New York, Mc Graw Hill Book Company.

Julia, H. 1983. Statistics for Economist, New Delhi. Heritage Publishers.

Kannan, K.P. 1995. Public Intervention and Poverty Alleviation : A Study of the Declining Incidence of Rural Poverty in Kerala. Development and Change, 26 (4) : 701-927.

Kumar, P. and Mathur, V.C. 1996. Agriculture in Future : Demand Supply Perspectives for the Ninth Five Plan. Economic and Political Weekly, 31 (39) : A131-A139.

Madnani, G.M.K., 1986. Introduction to Econometrics : Principles and Applications. Oxford and IBH Publishing Company.

Mahendra Dev, S. 1996. Food Security PDS vs. BGS : A tale of two States. Economic and Political Weekly, 31 (27) : 1752-1763.

Mehta, B.C., 1993. Region and Class Specific Determinants of Rural Poverty in India. Indian Journal of Regional Science, 25 (1) : 59-69.

Mishra, S.N., 1997. Agricultural Liberalization and Development Strategy in Ninth Plan. Economic and Political Weekly, 32 (13) : A10-A25.

Mishra, V.N., 1998. Economic Reforms, Terms of Trade, Aggregate Supply.

Mollah, H. 2002. Spectre of Drought Looming Large People's Democracy, Vol. 26, No. 33.

Pandey, V.K. and Sharma, K.C. 1996. Crop Diversification and Self Sufficiency in Foodgrains. Indian Journal of Agricultural Economics, 51 (4) : 644-651.

Parashar, A.K.; Singh, H.P. and Singh, S.P., 1980. Econometrics and Mathematical Economics, New Delhi, Sultan Chand and Company Ltd.

Radhakrishna, R., 1996. Food Trends, Public Distribution System and Food Security Concerns, Indian Journal of Agricultural Economics, 51 (1-2) : 168 : 183

Rana, R.P.S., 1982. Population and Food Supply : Need to Find New Methods of Growing Crops. Southern-Economist, 1st March, pp. 9-14.

Rao, V.K.R.V., 1982. Food Nutrition and Poverty in India, New Delhi. Vikas Publishing House.

Rao. V.M. 1993. The Wheat Story : Recent Changes in Price Policy. Economic and Price Policy. Economic and Political Weekly, 28 (44) : 2385-2386

Rawal, V. and Swaminathan, M. 1998. Changing Trajectories : Agricultural Growth in West Bengal, 1950 to 1996. Economic to Political Weekly. 33 (48) : 2595-2601.

Sarmishtha, P. and Pal, S. 1999. An analysis of Childhood Malnutrition in Rural India : Role of Gender, Income and Other Household Characteristics. World Development, 27 (7) : 1151-1171.

Satendra and Gupta, A. 2003. Managing Disaster must for Sustainable Management, Employment News, 25th-31st October.

Sawant, S.D. and Achuthan, C.V. 1995. Agricultural Growth Across Crops and Regions : Emerging Trends and Patterns. Economic and Political Weekly, 30 (10) : A2-A11.

Sawant, S.R., 1994. Inflation and Rural Poor. Economic and Political Weekly, 29 (9) : 483-485.

Shafi, M., 1984. Agricultural Productivity and Regional Imbalances, New Delhi. Concept Publishing House.

Shah, A., 1997. Food Security and Access to Natural Resources : A Review of Recent Trends. Economic and Political Weekly, 32 (26) : A47-A54.

Shantanu, N. and Nagpal, S., 1999. Food Security in Hindukush Himalyas, Economic and Political Weekly, 34 (38) : 2717-2720.

Shariff, A. and Mallick, A.C., 1999. Dynamics of Food Intake and Nutrition by Expenditure Class in India. Economic and Political Weekly, 34 (27) : 1790-1800.

Singh, G. and Bhogal, T.S. 2006. Food Security in Bihar : Key Issues and Strategies, Journal of Social and Economic Studies, 17 (1&2) : 1-15.

Singh, G. and Bhogal, T.S. 2006. Food Security Situation in Punjab : An Assessment, Southern Economist, 45 (2) : 18-20.

Singh, G. and Bhogal, T.S. 2006. Food Security Situation in Uttar Pradesh : An Assessment, Southern Economist, 45 (3) : 21-23.

Singh, G. and Bhogal, T.S., 2005. Food Security in the Haryana State : An Economic Analysis. Agricultural Marketing, 47 (1) : 28-35 (5).

Singh, G. and Bhogal, T.S., 2006. Assessment of Food Security Situation for Disaster Risk Management : An Analysis, for the Gujarat State, Anvesak, 45 (1) : 32-43.

Singh, G. and Bhogal, T.S., 2006. Food Security : An Assessment for the Tamilnadu State, Review of Development and Change, Vol. 11, No. 2, July-Dec.

Singh, G. and Bhogal, T.S., 2006. Food Security : Key Issues and Strategies for the Andhra Pradesh, Asian Economic Review, 48 (1) : 101-113.

Singh, G. and Bhogal, T.S., Food Security : Key Issues and Strategies for Kerala State – A Note, Indian Economic Review. (accepted paper).

Singh, G. and Bhogal, T.S., 2006. Food Security Situation in Karnataka : An Assessment, Southern Economist, 44 (21) : 17-10

Singh, G., 1997. Shortage of Wheat : Need to Improve Productivity. Southern Economist, 36 (9) : 7-10

Singh, I.J. 1998. Farm Poverty, Household Food Security and Agricultural Sustainability in India. Journal of Rural Development, 17 (4) : 619-631.

Singh, I.J.; Rai, K.N. and Karwesra, J.C. 1997. Regional Variations in Agricultural Performance in India. Indian Journal of Agricultural Economics, 5293) : 375-386.

Singh, L.P. 2004. Reforms with a Human Face : Public Distribution System Revisited, Employment News, 28th-3rd September.

Singh, S., 2004. Crises and Diversification in Punjab Agriculture : Role of State and Agribussiness, Economic and Political Weekly, Vol. 39, No. 52, Dec. 25-31, pp. 5583-5590.

Statistical Outline of India, 1999-2000. Tata Services Limited, Department of Economics and Statistics, Bombay House, Mumbai, p. 44.

Sullivan, G. and Claycombe, W.W., 1977. Fundamentals of Forecasting, Virginia, Reston Publishing Company.

Suman, S. and Sahai, S., 2000. Farmer's Right and Food Stamps. Economic and Political Weekly, 45 (11) : 878-880.

Suryanaryana, M.H., 1995. Some Experiments with Food Stamps. Economic and Political Weekly, 30 (51) : A151-A159.

***Swaminathan, M.S., 1986.** Building National and Global Nutrition Security Systems. Global Aspects of Food Production, eds. Swaminathan M.S. and Sinha, S.K., 417-449. (Natural Resources and Environment Series), Vol. 20. London : Tycooly Publishing.

Swaminathan, M.S., 1996. Science and Technology for Sustainable Food Security. Indian Journal of Agricultural Economics, 51 (1) : 60-75.

Taeuber, I.B., 1972. Population Growth and Development in South East Asia, in the Population Panel Seminars.

The Economic Times, 16th October, 1983, pp. 4-7.

The Employment News, dated 16-22 October, 2004.

The Financial Express, 6th December, 2001, p. 7.

The Hindu, 25th November, 1998, New Delhi.

The Hindustan Times, 22nd June, 2000, New Delhi.

Upadhyay, V., 1996. Inflation, Food Security and Public Distribution System. Social Action, 46 (3) : 296-308.

Various Years. Ministry of Agriculture, Directorate of Economics and Statistics. Indian Agriculture in Brief.

***Wolfenson, J.D., 1996.** Food Security for the World. An FAO World Food Summit, Rome, November, 1996. Proceedings, p. 12.

***World Bank, 1986.** Poverty and Hunger, Issues and Options for Food Security in Developing Countries, Washington D. C.

** References with asterisk (*) are not seen originally.*

Websites

www.ddsindia.com/approach paper, www.soils.usda.gov/use/worldsoils/ papers/food-security-asia, www.usaid.gov/policy/ads/200/pd19.pdf, www.fcamin.nic.in, www.fao.org (www.fao.org/docrep/005/Y4671E/y4671e00, www.fao.org/focus, www.un.org.in/Agencies/fao), www.mohfw.nic.in /natpp, www.tn.gov.in/policynotes/agri2004-05, www.agricoop.nic.in/prices new.htm-14k, www.ryerson.ca/foodsec/centre, www.indiabudget.nic.in., www.indiatogether.org/2004/jan/pov-keralapds.htm, pib.nic.in.

www.ciionline.org/northern/ regionalfocus, www.cidi.org/disaster, www.riverlinks.nic.in, www.fivims.org, planning commission.nic.in/aboutus/committee/wrkgrp/agriallied.

Appendix 2 : State wise Population Projections* from 1996 to 2011.

(in millions)

S.No.	*States/Year*	*1996*	*2001*	*2006*	*2011*
1.	Andhra Pradesh	72.2	76.4	80.6	84.8
2.	Assam	24.7	26.5	28.4	30.5
3.	Bihar	93.0	101.8	111.1	121.3
4.	Gujarat	45.5	49.0	52.5	56.1
5.	Haryana	18.5	20.1	21.7	23.4
6.	Himachal Pradesh	6.0	6.8	7.5	7.9
7.	Jammu and Kashmir	8.9	10.1	11.1	11.6
8.	Karnataka	49.3	52.7	56.2	59.6
9.	Kerala	31.0	32.5	34.2	35.6
10.	Madhya Pradesh	74.2	81.2	88.6	96.6
11.	Maharashtra	86.6	92.1	97.3	102.6
12.	Orissa	34.4	36.2	37.8	39.5
13.	Punjab	22.4	23.8	25.3	26.7
14.	Rajasthan	49.7	54.5	59.6	65.3
15.	Tamil Nadu	59.4	62.2	65.0	67.6
16.	Uttar Pradesh	156.7	174.3	194.1	217.1
17.	West Bengal	74.6	79.9	85.4	90.8

Note: 1. Projection Based on Sample Registration Systems by the Technical Group, 1996, Registrar General, India, Using 1996 as the Base Year.

2. The Population Projection Figures is for the Major States Selected for the Study.

*As on I st March of the year

Source: Statistical Out line of India, 1999-2000. Tata Services Limited, Department of Economics and Statistics, Bombay House, Mumbai, p. 44.

APPENDICES

Appendix 1 : Balanced Diet Requirement* by Age groups for Different Food Stuffs.

Age Group	*Adult Man*			*Adult Women*			*Children*		*Boys*	*Girls*
	Sedentary	*Moderate work*	*Heavy work*	*Sedentary*	*Moderate work*	*Heavy work*	*1-3 Years*	*4-6 Years*	*10-12 Years*	*10-12 Years*
Cereals	460	520	670	410	440	575	175	270	420	380
Pulses	40	50	60	40	45	50	35	35	45	45
Leafy Vegetables	40	40	40	100	100	50	40	50	50	50
Other Vegetables	60	70	80	40	40	100	20	30	50	50
Roots and Tubers	50	60	80	50	50	60	10	20	30	30
Milk	150	200	250	100	150	200	300	250	250	250
Oils and Fats	40	45	65	20	25	40	15	25	40	35
Sugar and Jaggery	30	35	55	20	20	40	30	40	45	45

* Grams per day for each category.

Source: ICMR, 1984